My Private War

Relentlessly Chasing a Dream—
From the Navy to the Major Leagues

Mitch Harris

To those who encouraged me — thank you.
To those who doubted me — thank you.

To Rylan and Camden:

This book is for you. Every struggle, every step forward, every moment I kept going—it was all for you. Even in my darkest days, I fought to become the kind of father you could look up to. My hope is that within these pages, you'll see what's possible when you refuse to quit, when you believe in something bigger, and when you trust that God is always at work—even when it's hard to see. You are braver, stronger, and more capable than you know. I'm proud to be your Dad. I love you.

To Mandi:

You are my rock. Your quiet strength, steady love, and relentless belief carried me through more than you know. You stood strong when I couldn't. You loved me through every high and low. Your independence, grace, and grit were exactly what I needed. Thank you for being you. I love you.

Contents

Introduction

A DREAM CAN BE a powerful life force. It can motivate you, tantalize you, and break your heart. I speak from personal experience. Mine took me to hell and back.

You may know about my triumphant moment. It was in all the papers. Perhaps you watched it live on television.

On the evening of April 25, 2015, I started walking from the visiting bullpen to the pitcher's mound at Milwaukee's Miller Park, and my future wife started crying. Because she understood what the moment meant to me.

At the ripe old age of twenty-nine, I made my debut appearance as a relief pitcher for the St. Louis Cardinals, becoming the first Naval Academy graduate to play in the Major Leagues in ninety-four years.

It was a proud moment for the Navy and the Cardinals, two institutions that remain close to my heart.

Baseball celebrated the unique achievement and my unlikely road to the bigs after five years away from the game, five years spent serving my country as a Naval officer, with three deployments including a combat tour during Operation Iraqi Freedom.

All these years later, some people see me as an inspirational figure, as a fastball-throwing embodiment of the American Dream.

The staggering odds I overcame to realize my lifelong ambition will hopefully inspire any person who dares to think big.

Impossible is just a word, and I'm living proof.

Time after time, I stared down impossible and kept chasing my dream.

But this is not merely a book about the magnificent view from a career summit.

It's also about struggle, doubt, and heartache, and you need to know the rest of the story.

How most college baseball programs rejected me coming out of high school.

How the Navy repeatedly rebuffed my appeals to play baseball while on active duty.

How my arm grew old and slow.

How the one person I then loved the most in this world insisted I was wasting my time.

But my dream had a heartbeat all its own, and I kept relentlessly chasing it, into the darkness and then into the light.

Every dream worth pursuing ultimately exacts a high price, and to truly appreciate my career as a big-league pitcher, you must understand the private war I fought to achieve it—not just against the military bureaucracy and the ravages of time, but against my own demons.

In my darkest hour, I even wondered if God had abandoned me.

On that fraught night, I walked into the shadows carrying a loaded gun.

Just about then, God showed up.

1

Where the Dream Began

MY FATHER WAS INSTRUMENTAL in developing my love of baseball. He spent ample time with me in the backyard, working on my mechanics and instructing me on the fundamentals.

Many afternoons, Mom would look out from the kitchen, where she was cooking dinner, and see a familiar sight: a crouching dad encouraging his son to hit the leather target.

Around five years old, I hit a milestone. It was 1990, and our family had recently moved from Anderson, South Carolina, to Lawrenceville, Georgia, in metro Atlanta's bustling Gwinnett County. I had just started playing tee-ball.

We stood on the tee-ball field, and Dad, who helped coach the team, saw an opportunity to teach me a lesson.

"Hey, Mitch, did you know that you can get the ball, step on second, and throw it to first and get two outs?"

He could see my little mind trying to process this baseball logic for the first time.

"Hey, Mitch, did you know that if there's a runner on first and second and you're playing third base, if you catch the ball and step on third and throw it to second and he goes to first, you get three outs?"

It was a common father-son moment, negotiated in various ways by every boy who starts playing baseball and slowly learns the rules and nuances of the game.

I got real quiet, the wheels turning in my mind, and a few moments later, raced up to my dad with my latest discovery. "Dad, did you know if the bases were loaded and somebody hits the ball to the pitcher, he can touch home, throw it to third and..."

Dad smiled and shook his head. "Mitch," he said, "you can't get four outs."

But I was thinking—desperately trying to figure out the language that defined my new little world.

Some moments offer a hint of the man you will become. From an early age, thanks to my dad's patient teaching, I started to understand that excelling in sports required more than talent and aggression.

Cy Harris was an only child, and although I eventually had two younger sisters, being the only boy created a special bond between us. We've always been close. In many ways, he was my best friend. I always felt like I could talk to him about anything.

Dad and my mom, Cindy, had met as undergraduates at Lee University, a small Christian college in Cleveland, Tennessee. They married right after graduation and moved to Ocala, Florida, where Dad started his career as a music minister for the Church of God. I was born on November 7, 1985, and in time, Mom began work as an accountant while also keeping house and becoming deeply involved with the numerous church events.

Looking back on my childhood, it was rather idyllic. We weren't rich by any means, but we never wanted for any necessities, and my wonderful mom always took great pains to do special things for all of us, even if it meant she had to do without something for herself. Now I know that she frequently scrimped to give us the little extras.

I knew my parents loved us more than anything in the world, and it's hard to overstate the importance of love and stability during those formative years. They gave us a strong foundation of traditional values. We were taught to live by the Golden Rule, to treat people the way we would want to be treated, and I always felt a special responsibility to measure up to expectations, keep my nose clean, and set a good example for my younger sisters.

Every father lives vicariously through his son's exploits, and mine was no different. Dad had been an athlete in high school, and it was clear from an early age, that he wanted me to be athletic.

He sure wasn't going to let me be a couch potato.

Many times he walked through the house on a Saturday or a lazy summer afternoon, saw me playing Nintendo, switched off the video game, and told me to go outside.

Soon I learned that he didn't really care what I did—as long as I was out in the fresh air. He knew I would invariably wind up playing baseball or basketball in the yard.

Still, he didn't push me into sports. But he didn't coddle me either.

Competitiveness is a mysterious quality, and my father carefully cultivated a competitive streak in me.

When we went out to play one-on-one basketball in our backyard, he would try to block my shot and vigorously defend my dribble. He never took it easy on me.

The same could be said for our frequent golf outings. Dad was a low-handicap golfer, and we spent a lot of time together on the links. As I moved into my teenage years and started getting pretty good with a golf club, I used to ask him: "What would you do if I ever beat you out here?"

His standard reply: "I'd let you find another ride home."

This was our running joke, but sometimes I wasn't sure if he was joking, which just filled me with an even greater desire to somehow, someday beat him.

Even as a young boy, I hated to lose.

Hated it.

So, when I lost, I practiced harder and played harder, reinforcing a life lesson from the old man's parenting master plan.

We wound up moving several times, as Dad felt led to different churches, but the center of our universe was always the church. If the doors were open, we were there. Many of my best friends came out of those various activities, which probably kept me out of trouble.

When you grow up in the church, you either rebel against all that tension between right and wrong, or you see God as a forgiving and gracious father. I always felt the comforting peace of God's love, and never really rebelled, at least partially because I was intently focused on my budding athletic career.

By the ripe old age of ten, I had it all planned: I was going to play for the Atlanta Braves.

Of course, I was not yet acquainted with a rather daunting math problem: Making it to the big leagues is only slightly less probable than being struck by lightning.

It was a magical time to be a Braves fan, as manager Bobby Cox led the once-lowly franchise to a Major League–record fourteen consecutive division titles starting in 1991, negotiating the improbable turnaround from worst to first. No one stood taller to me than right-handed starting pitcher John Smoltz, the eight-time All-Star and future Hall of Famer. Smoltz was a beast, and he struck fear into the hearts of opposing batters, propelled by a combination of power and finesse.

Those were some amazing teams. The Braves featured two other future Hall of Fame pitchers: Greg Maddux and Tom Glavine. Legendary position players including Chipper Jones, David Justice, and Sid Bream always came up with clutch hits.

More often than not, the good guys won, and the next day at school, it was all we wanted to talk about.

Sure, we were disappointed time and again in the playoffs, but the 1995 World Series victory over Cleveland still ranks as one of the greatest moments in Atlanta sports history.

And did I mention those fourteen straight division titles?

Especially in those days, when the winning was new, when Atlanta had finally, after all those dreadful years, allowed itself to believe in the Braves, so many of us felt like we were taking this incredible ride together.

The specifics escape me, but I attended my first Braves game when the team still played at aging Atlanta-Fulton County Stadium. Stashed away somewhere in my parents' attic is a prized Bat Day bat and various other mementos from those days. We attended games often, especially after the team moved to sparkling new Turner Field, which felt like a palace. I was the skinny kid with the goofy grin.

I can close my eyes and still feel the excitement of those electric moments, watching those heroic figures do amazing things. Ryan Klesko blasting a powerful home run. Marquis Grissom chasing down a long ball in centerfield. Jeff Blauser scooping up a ground ball, flipping it to Mark Lemke, who tossed to Fred McGriff for a 6-4-3 double play. They made it look so easy.

Carefully studying Smoltz as he warmed up was a particular treat, and when he got some enemy batter to bite on a fading breaking ball for yet another K, no one cheered louder than his little buddy Mitch, who often found himself dreaming about the future.

How awesome would it be to do this for my career?

To put on a uniform and go out and play baseball for my job?

I could be the guy that kids like me look up to and want to be like!

Even then, I was thinking through the prism of the baseball player as a role model.

I enjoyed playing several different sports and was a good basketball player. But baseball was my passion.

We had a big backyard with a fence. During the summer, Dad would mow out a place for base paths, and we would install little rubber bases. That's where my friends and I would play, often utilizing tennis balls and one of those little souvenir bats I acquired during one of my trips to Turner Field.

The sweet spot was tiny but you could hit a tennis ball a mile with one of those little bats, often into the distant trees.

Even as I began to attract attention as both pitcher and hitter in the youth leagues, I spent most of my time playing baseball in my head, leaning on my encyclopedic knowledge of all the National League starting lineups, gleaned through meticulous reading of newspapers and magazines.

Our house in Lawrenceville had a long driveway, and a cement wall framed the whole left side. I would tape a square on the wall and pitch a tennis ball into it, pretending to be Smoltz, bringing the heat and striking out the side.

Someday, I just knew I would make that triumphant walk to the mound at Turner Field, as the massive crowd of Tomahawk Choppers went wild.

Someday.

Focused like a laser on hitting my imaginary cement strike zone, I provided my own running commentary, which echoed down the street.

Oh my! Did you see that heater from Harris?

The pride of Lawrenceville, Georgia!

Look at Sammy Sosa's face! He can't believe he just took a called third strike from Rookie of the Year Mitch Harris!

I wasn't just playing the game in my mind.

Like many American boys, I was starting to chase an idea that cut straight to the heart of our shared culture—a dream that would prove more elusive than I could possibly imagine.

***

Playing recreation league baseball was primarily about having fun, but it was also the first step in learning how to compete—against other players and with myself.

"Mitch was always one of the best players but he wasn't head-and-shoulders above everybody else, and I think that was important," Mom said. "He was never in a situation where he didn't have to work hard."

One time Dad got irritated because I was moping around after making a mistake and wasn't cheering for my teammates. So he benched me, which surprised the head coach.

"What are you doing? He's our best player!"

"I don't care," my dad insisted. "He wasn't doing right and he needs to learn a lesson."

Only later would I appreciate how difficult this must have been for my dad. The path of least resistance in that situation is to let the kid play, especially to keep the rest of the team from suffering. But he was right. I needed to learn a lesson about bringing the right attitude to the ballpark, and I carry it to this day, long after my baseball days.

The close relationship with my father helped me negotiate a thorny problem early in my high school years.

Dad was a gifted and dedicated music minister, and he was determined to bring a championship effort to our worship program. Our church featured a large choir and a full orchestra, which produced a powerful sound that filled up the sanctuary. Everyone felt God's presence when all those voices meshed perfectly together.

Mom sang in the choir, and at one point during middle school, I was recruited to fill a need in the brass section.

"I need a good trombone player," Dad said. "You're it."

It was not a request.

In addition to Sunday and Wednesday services, I devoted at least one more night of the week to orchestra rehearsal, not to mention learning my music and practicing at home. While I actually enjoyed playing music, the trombone soon became a lead weight dangling from my socially insecure teenage neck.

By the time I got into high school, my ego was taking a real beating. I was pretty serious about being an athlete, and playing the trombone was not cool. Eventually I pulled Dad aside for one of our heart-to-heart talks, and he understood my choice to prioritize baseball.

It helped that he was so involved in my budding athletic career.

Like most red-blooded Southern boys, I loved football but Dad put his foot down.

He likes to tell the story of seeing my friends in middle school head off to football practice while I lingered behind the fence, with a rather forlorn look.

"Mr. Harris, why won't you let your son play football?"

"I just can't do it. I got too many kids at the church. Every time I see 'em, something's dangling. I just can't let him play. It's a gut feeling."

Though he feared I would get hurt playing football, he also once admonished me for not being aggressive enough on the basketball court. Perhaps he was right because the refs rarely tagged me with a foul. I probably defended and drove the lane too tentatively. "If you don't start getting some fouls," he said, "I'm taking you off the team."

I desperately wanted to stay on the team, and he knew it.

Taking the criticism to heart, I stepped on the court that night with a more aggressive attitude and the refs quickly took notice, calling my number twice within a matter of minutes. Looking out to my dad in the stands, I gave him a shrug and flashed a funny face, as if to say, "Happy now?"

Over several years, Dad and the other coaches helped me improve my baseball mechanics as my body slowly matured, and I consistently made the youth league All-Stars, selected by the coaches. But high school was a whole new deal, and there was only so much that the music minister and his friends could teach me.

One day during my sophomore year, he sat me down and said, "Mitch, you're playing several sports. If you had to choose, which sport would you choose?"

By this time, Dad had taken a new job, and we had moved to Mount Holly, North Carolina. I was playing varsity basketball at South Point High School in Belmont, the sixth man guard on a good team.

But the choice between basketball and baseball was easy.

Of course, baseball was my true love. Dad knew this without asking but wanted to give me the responsibility of choosing, because being invited to join a highly regarded travel baseball team was a big deal and represented a major commitment in both money and time for my parents.

"If we're going to do this, I want you to make a commitment, and your mom and I will support you in your decision," he said.

It was essentially my first adult decision, even before I owned a driver's license, and the choice was destined to reverberate through my life.

All the guys on that team were good, and the competition really pushed me.

So now I was a 100-percent baseball player, and something about making this very conscious choice filled me with renewed purpose. No longer was I just playing youth sports. I was chasing a career.

It felt like I was truly heading somewhere special, and this feeling had a lot to do with my new travel ball coach.

Gary Robinson had been a scout for the Montreal Expos, and I learned so much about training and mechanics from him.

As a pitching staff, we ran through the Expos' warm-up program, which proved to be a tremendous step forward in my development, as I began to learn how to control my arm in a whole new way.

Through Gary's coaching, baseball became more than a game to me. It wasn't just about having fun anymore. Every pitch had intent. Every swing meant something. I started to see the game within the game.

***

When I speak to groups about making it to the big leagues, I always like to point out a few universal truths.

You can be an extremely hard worker—and not make it.

You can have a terrible work ethic—and still make it.

And you can have all the talent in the world—and not make it.

There are athletes blessed with 4.3 speed who never truly make it in football for one reason or another, and there are guys who can crush a fastball a mile but can't hit a curveball. Most of them are selling insurance.

Talent gives you a chance, but it's only one piece of a complex puzzle.

The formula for achieving success is different for everyone, and realizing a professional sports dream depends on so many variables.

I was blessed with a good amount of talent, but early on realized that I needed a strong work ethic to have a chance to get to the next level.

Mickey Lineberger, the head baseball coach at South Point High School, was the first person to really challenge me in ways that made me a better ball player.

He recognized my athleticism in my freshman year, tried to envision what I could become by the time I graduated, and carefully guided me to reach my potential.

Looking back on those days now, without the combination of Robinson and Lineberger, I don't think you would be reading my book or care the least bit about my story. It would take many breaks for me to make it, and solid coaching during those years factored into my ultimate success. Those two men helped me become the man I desperately wanted to be.

After enjoying a good year on the junior varsity team as a freshman—pitching and playing third base—I was crushed when Coach Lineberger didn't elevate me to the varsity team as a sophomore.

What did I have to do?

Did he have something against me?

His decision hit me hard, and I calmly shared my frustrations with Lineberger as well as my father.

"It was difficult for Mitch to see the big picture," Dad said.

Lineberger assured me that the every-day reps I would get on the JV team would allow me to improve, as opposed to riding the bench most of the time with the varsity, and he was right. He knew what I needed, and when I needed it. Out of this experience I learned humility and patience, and without a doubt, all that B-team action transformed me into a much better player by the time I made the varsity roster as a junior.

"You could see Mitch gaining confidence in himself, not just as an athlete but also as a young man," Dad said.

In both 2003 and 2004, pitching, playing third base, and hitting over .400, I earned all-conference and all-state honors. It felt like I was clicking on all cylinders.

We had some outstanding players at South Point in those days. Two of my teammates—Matt Camp and Devon Lowery—were drafted out of high school, and several others signed college scholarships.

The thought of playing at the next level started to feel real, like something I could reach out and touch.

I knew I wasn't good enough to be drafted—not then, with a fastball in the mid-80s—but went into the process hoping for a Division I scholarship, which would take a load off my parents financially and eventually get me in front of professional scouts. Attending several college camps introduced me to a new level of evaluation, but the coach at North Carolina State insisted I wasn't ready for the Atlantic Coast Conference and recommended that I go to a junior college and finish growing.

This experience was a blow. On the one hand, the coach could see I had potential and actually talked about the possibility that I could mature into that sort of world in a couple of years. Who knew how big and strong I might be by then? But patience didn't come easily for me, and at a time when I was a good high school athlete, patted on the back for being a South Point hero, it was difficult to understand that it was a huge leap to the next level.

Welcome to the real world, Mitch.

Adjusting my sights, I began to look at Division II and NAIA programs. The thought of using baseball to earn a college education at a small school like Gardner Webb, Lenoir-Rhyne, or Elon became a big motivator. Lee University, my parents' alma mater, offered me a scholarship, but the thought of being so close to my paternal grandparents was not necessarily a selling point. I was eager to be on my own.

If I could land a scholarship to a smaller college, perhaps in time I could transfer to a bigger school. Maybe my future was as a slugging infielder and not a pitcher. So many possibilities ran through my mind during those hopeful but uncertain days.

At times, it occurred to me that maybe I was deluding myself about playing professionally, but I usually kept this doubtful narrative buried deep, where it could not dent my confidence. The dream was still very much alive in my beating heart.

Then Davidson started pursuing me.

In the autumn of 2003, I took an official visit with my parents to the elite North Carolina liberal arts college, often ranked academically in a class with Duke and Vanderbilt. The Wildcats played in the Division I Southern Conference, alongside rivals including Appalachian State, Tennessee-Chattanooga, and The Citadel. I fell in love with the charming little campus, with an enrollment smaller than many high schools. It felt like home.

After visiting with members of the team, I whispered to Dad, "Some of those guys were talking about the stock market."

Baseball wasn't the most important thing in this rarefied air, but the coach wanted me and went to bat for me with the admissions people. My grades were pretty good—mostly As, with a sprinkling of Bs—and everything we were told was positive.

When the admissions envelope arrived, I nervously ripped it open, while sitting at the kitchen table with my folks.

My heart sank.

It was a rejection letter.

Apparently, my grades were not good enough.

"That was a crushing blow for Mitch," Mom said. "They had pursued him, and he had gotten his hopes up."

I was pretty devastated, wondering if my dream was slipping away.

With my senior year of high school baseball approaching, no other Division I program was interested in me. Not a single one.

2

Course Correction

THE DAVIDSON REJECTION WAS a punch in the gut.

Because they had pursued me so aggressively.

Because we had already started making so many plans.

When will you be leaving to go to Davidson, Mitch?

What will you need for your dorm room?

We were already *that* invested. It felt like a done deal.

And then it just slipped away.

Sitting at the kitchen table, as we all learned the difficult truth, I could tell Mom and Dad were worried about how I would react.

"Are you okay?" Mom asked sweetly.

The look of concern on Dad's face is frozen in my mind.

Now that I'm a parent, I can look back on that situation with a little more perspective.

As a parent, you would do anything in the world to protect your child from any sort of harm, including heartbreak. This is a pretty primal force. And yet, along the way, you also realize that this impulse inevitably conflicts with various facts of life.

My parents couldn't protect me from that disappointment any more than they could shield me from a skinned knee. Pain is part of life, and if you don't get hurt, you aren't really living.

Becoming an adult means learning to deal with all sorts of setbacks, and looking back on it now, I started to negotiate an important passage toward adulthood with the Davidson experience.

There were plenty of tough days to come in my life. I was going to need some pretty thick skin.

Of course I was disappointed, ticked off, hurt even, but after the initial shock, a rather surprising calm came over me. Even now, it's difficult for me to explain why.

"It is what it is," I told my parents. "For whatever reason, I've got this peace about it. I guess that wasn't where I was supposed to go."

Mom just looked at me and said nothing for a moment or two.

My measured reaction floored them.

"Mitch showed real maturity," Mom said. "He handled that situation very well. It looked like that might be his only real chance, and yet he didn't allow it to get him down. He kept thinking there was going to be another option."

It was more blind faith than confidence.

Even then, I just felt that there was a professional baseball player trapped inside me, trying to get out. Nobody could see him except me.

Truthfully, my options to continue playing baseball were limited.

I probably would have wound up at Gardner-Webb or a junior college, hoping that I matured into a Division I prospect.

It was hard for me to tell whether those coaches, who turned me down by saying that I wasn't quite mature enough, were just blowing smoke or being sincere. Maybe some of them thought I just wasn't good enough and never would be—and maybe they were right. There was no way to know who I might be in two or three years.

No one in the SEC or ACC was banging down my door, but my dream of reaching a higher level still lived on inside me, even as I tried to enjoy my senior year at South Point.

As my high school career drew to a close and I finished a great season, I could look back with appreciation on Coach Lineberger's wisdom. Impatience can be a good thing and a bad thing in an athlete. You need some juice inside you, but you also need to see the big picture without pushing too hard. He had been right to urge patience at just the right time. I became a better player because of the way he handled me.

How I loved the game, especially those tense moments when I released the ball out of my hand and flung it into a spinning, 60-foot, 6-inch universe of action and reaction. Those moments made sense to me. There was something simple and empowering about pushing away all the other distractions in my complicated teenage life to concentrate on competing with another human being who was waiting for me to throw my best punch and determined to throw his best punch back.

It didn't matter if I was trying to overpower him with my fastball, which honestly wasn't very fast in those days, or fool him with a breaking pitch on the outside corner. I was pushing hard against my own potential, trying to figure out how to best leverage my natural talent and the skills and knowledge I had developed through the years, synthesizing all of that coaching and applied intelligence. Me against the batter. Me against me.

Of course, in those days, I was a much better hitter, and taking some guy deep was always a great thrill. Is there a better feeling than being eighteen and watching the ball you just crushed sail over the distant fence as your teammates and friends cheer?

How alive this made me feel.

That spring, I soaked up every moment of sheer joy.

Every so often, in rare moments of doubt, I allowed myself to wonder, *What if this is my last year of baseball?*

What if it ends here?

***

We all face turning points. Something unexpected happens, and it takes your life in one direction or another, leading you toward your destiny. Often it can be difficult to appreciate the full significance of one specific event until you gain a little distance from it and can trace the tumbling dominos.

One turning point in my life led to so many others.

My life pivoted on the day James "Buddy" Green stumbled into it, propelling me toward a very different reality.

I knew it then.

I appreciate it even more today.

Without his unlikely intervention in my life, it is doubtful you would be reading this book.

One day during my senior year, in the spring of 2004, Green visited my high school. By this time, he had spent more than two decades as a college football coach, including stops at LSU, Auburn, and N.C. State and a six-year stint as head coach at Tennessee-Chattanooga. He was in his third year as defensive coordinator for the United States Naval Academy, and stopped by South Point on a football recruiting trip.

I happened to be throwing in the bullpen before our game that day. Green, who had planned to meet Coach Lineberger, who was also the assistant football coach, walked up and started looking me over.

One thing led to another, and he started asking questions about me:

"How are his grades? What sort of kid is he? Would he ever consider a service academy?"

When he introduced himself to me, I was confused. *Why would someone from the Navy want to talk with me about baseball?*

To be honest, I didn't know anything about the Naval Academy, and when I got home that night and tried to explain the situation to my parents, they felt suddenly confused and concerned. Less than three years after the 9/11 terrorist attacks, the United States was in the middle of bloody wars in Afghanistan and Iraq. When I said "Navy," Mom assumed the man was recruiting for the fleet, sniffing around looking for warm bodies to ship off to the front.

"Tell them you're not interested, and don't sign anything!" Mom insisted.

She knew things that I didn't.

But I kept pitching.

"No, Mom, that's not what this is..."

After I carefully relayed my conversation with the man, the wheels began to turn in Mom's head. "Wait a minute. Do you mean to tell me that someone came to the high school today to talk to you about playing baseball at Annapolis?"

I was more confused than she was. "Well, I guess."

Annapolis?

I didn't know what Annapolis was or why the word had surprised and impressed my mom so much.

A day or two later, when one of the Navy baseball coaches called to talk with me, I still struggled to process what the Naval Academy was and how baseball fit into the equation. But slowly I began to understand what a prestigious institution the Naval Academy is and the remarkable opportunity that was being dangled before me.

"Suddenly, it was like somebody from the Ivy League showing an interest in Mitch," Mom recalled.

This was rather bizarre on two levels. First of all, I had been repeatedly told I wasn't good enough to play Division I baseball. And Navy competes in the highest NCAA division, albeit with something of an asterisk befitting the hybrid circumstances of the service academies.

The strange twist of fate that caused this football coach, out recruiting football players, to visit my school, and then plan to meet at the baseball field prior to walking over to football practice, was difficult to comprehend. The Navy baseball coaches never even saw me pitch. Not once. The high school scouting resources weren't so sophisticated then, and coaches didn't rely so heavily on services provided by *Baseball America*, *Perfect Game*, or *Prep Baseball Report*. Apparently, the Navy coaches called some of the coaches in our area and checked out my stats but mostly, they just took Green's word that I might be good enough to make their team, and next thing I knew, we were taking an official visit.

It all happened so fast, my head was spinning.

Was I now a Division I prospect? Or had the stars just aligned to give me a chance to be recruited to a unique place that didn't really recruit?

On a cold and dreary spring day, my parents and I visited Annapolis, a quaint little town in Maryland on the western shore of Chesapeake Bay.

The aura of the Academy, founded in 1845, hit me in the gut. You could feel the history. But the spartan and run-down baseball facilities caught us by surprise.

"Oh, it was so miserable, and we went to a game and were three of maybe ten people in the stands," Dad said.

Mom recalled the "old wooden bleachers, looked like you might fall through if you weren't careful. I mean, it was not very impressive."

It didn't take us long to understand that baseball and the other sports didn't wield the same sort of clout at the Naval Academy as they do at other major schools, but we all came away incredibly impressed by the storied institution and the opportunity to earn a first-class education.

After one of the coaches walked me through the process, I faced a defining decision.

As I began to learn about the rich history of the Academy, and to understand that Midshipmen received a free education at one of the most prestigious colleges in America in return for a five-year commitment to the Navy after graduation, something began to stir inside me.

While both my grandfathers served in World War II—my mother's father had been enlisted in the Army, and my dad's father, the Navy—we didn't have any modern-day ties to the military and certainly didn't know any high-ranking military officers. But the idea of serving my country intrigued me, especially in the wake of 9/11, as a new wave of patriotism surged through my generation.

By the time we got home, the decision weighed heavily on my mind. This was way bigger than choosing a college, way bigger than grabbing the precious opportunity to play college baseball. It was a huge commitment that would change the course of my life.

Mom and Dad understood this from the start. It took me a while.

The mother who initially insisted that I avoid talking to anyone from the Navy understood that the Army, Navy, Air Force, and Marines routinely recruited graduating high school seniors to start at the bottom in the enlisted ranks, and of course, this was a good option for many individuals who went on to outstanding military careers. She was afraid of me signing away my life and never getting the chance to go to college.

But Mom's attitude changed, and it had nothing to do with baseball.

"Of course, it was great that Mitch would get to play baseball, and I was happy about that," she said. "But going to Annapolis? I thought if he went to Annapolis and was able to get that sort of education and become an officer in the Navy, he would be set for life. I thought it would create a whole new set of possibilities. A whole new world would open up for him."

However, it also meant that I might die in service to my country.

When you're eighteen, you think you're bulletproof. You don't think about death. But I had to consider it. Very carefully.

"What do you think?" I asked Dad during a private moment. "Should I do this?"

Pointing to the floor, he said, "You need to get on your knees."

My faith served as a huge anchor in my life. I definitely needed to talk with God about this big decision.

Over the next week or so, we all prayed and discussed the various pros and cons.

There were some pretty sober moments as we discussed the situation, and I was fully aware of what I was choosing. In the end, my heart was sure.

When I told my parents I had decided to go to the Naval Academy, they supported me without question.

In reality, the process was just starting.

When the phone book–size official application arrived in the mail, Dad remarked, "It's like we're doing this whole thing backwards."

Out of this process, I first learned about the honor code.

What do you mean if you lie, you can get kicked out? Really? A little white lie, and you're gone?

Throughout my childhood and adolescence, my parents had consistently modeled the importance of living a life of character and integrity.

Dad often said, "Only you can control your character and integrity. Nobody can take that away from you. A big piece of that is that your word has to mean something. If your reputation is ever taken from you, it's because you allow it to happen."

At this critical juncture especially, he took the time to emphasize the stakes of choosing Annapolis. "If you're going to go to the Naval Academy, you need to know what you're signing up for, and what you are making a commitment to do."

The application packet included a series of rigorous academic and physical tests I needed to administer myself, all while bound by the honor code, including completing a certain number of pull-ups and sit-ups in a specified time as well as a basketball toss. You had to get on your knees and throw a basketball as far as you could, without falling forward, and then record the distance.

With the clock ticking, I faced two huge obstacles.

Ordinarily, a prospective student must receive a coveted appointment to one of the service academies by a member of the House of Representatives or the Senate. Because this happened during the spring of my senior year, all of the Congressional appointments from the North Carolina delegation had been taken.

"What do we do now?" Dad asked the Navy coach during one plaintive phone call, trying to work the problem.

"Let me see what I can do."

The Navy coaches wanted me, but they made it clear: I had to get myself in.

A complicated process followed over the next several weeks.

What if the opportunity disappears before my eyes, like Davidson?

Believe me, this thought lingered in my mind.

I'm still not sure how they worked it out, but apparently the baseball coach convinced the commandant to use one of his precious administrative appointments to get me in, way past the usual time. To say I was lucky in all this would be a tremendous understatement.

But on that day in June 2004, when I reported to Annapolis and became a lowly plebe, surrendering complete control of my life, I didn't fully appreciate that I was stepping into a future that would enable my greatest dream—and, at the same time, threaten it.

3

Losing Control

SOME OF MY CLASSMATES saw the Naval Academy as a prison.

Believe me, they took hold of your life.

Especially during plebe year, when the system takes great pains to make you understand that you are the lowest of the low, it was easy to feel trapped, beleaguered, and desperate.

The trick was to understand that they *wanted* you to feel trapped, beleaguered, and desperate.

It was all part of the training to become a Naval officer.

It was all part of learning to lead, protect, and never give up the ship.

Not everyone was cut out for the unrelenting pressure of the place, and some of my classmates dropped out, especially during that harrowing first year.

That first day of Plebe Summer, I wasn't so sure what I had gotten myself into—or if I would survive long enough to earn my precious ensign's bars.

I Day—Induction Day—is one I will never forget.

Mom and Dad flew up to Baltimore with me, and then we rented a car and drove to Annapolis, where I joined the long line of plebes headed into registration at Alumni Hall, carrying only a duffel bag.

Once inside, you suddenly had to memorize your all-important identifying alpha code and were given a booklet they called Reef Points, which told all sorts of facts about the Naval Academy and the American military. It didn't take me long to understand that every Midshipman would be expected to learn every conceivable nugget contained in this informative little booklet and then regurgitate it on demand. I learned to study it like the book of Proverbs.

Not long after I moved on to the next station of the induction line, up a flight of stairs inside the ancient gymnasium, waiting my turn, some officer ran up to me and started blessing me out for not using my free time wisely.

"Up against that wall!"

"Start reading your Reef Points!"

"Ninety-degree angle!"

Seriously? This guy is screaming at me because I need to read a book when I'm waiting in line?

I'd been at the Academy maybe ten minutes and was already getting chewed out.

Of course they wanted to get us flustered. It was all part of the deal. My butt belonged to the Navy now, and God help me if some officer or upperclassman asked for my alpha code and I couldn't spit it out instantly.

After they fitted me for my uniform, tennis shoes, and cover; administered some shots; drew some blood; and gave me a buzz cut, I followed the crowd out the door to meet a bus, which would take me to my new home, the storied Bancroft Hall. I was carrying a bag filled with all of my new worldly possessions, courtesy of the American taxpayer.

The duffel bag I had been told to bring to campus with some clothes and personal items? It had been confiscated on the way into Alumni Hall. I wouldn't see it again for months.

While we waited for the bus, an officer started teaching a small group of us how to salute, barking instructions and jumping on anybody who didn't do it right.

"Look at me!"

"Slight angle!"

"Ninety-degree!"

"Just above your eye!"

Some of us got it right away and some of us needed some help.

"No! Like this!"

"Watch me! Like this!"

On the bus, we were all reading Reef Points at attention, feeling the quickly mounting tension of the moment deep in our guts.

You didn't want to give one of the upper-class superiors (known as "cadres") any excuse to approach you.

Just let me blend in while I study this booklet.

Okay, the Academy was founded when? What's the third enlisted rank in the Navy?

And what's my number?

On the way into Bancroft, I learned that the Academy had assigned me to Company H, or Hotel Company as we called it, which meant that I would be living on the first floor. The entire brigade of about 4,000 was housed in the massive dormitory.

This is where "chopping" came into my life.

A plebe anywhere in Bancroft had to jog in a precise march known as the high-knee, or "chop," in the middle of the hallway and on the right side of the stairs. And if an upperclassman told you to "hit the bulkhead," you were expected to press your sorry butt against the wall at attention and start reciting your personal details, while of course studying your Reef Points.

"Yes, sir," "Go Navy, sir," and "Beat Army, sir," were quickly drilled into our collective consciousness, appropriate for just about any situation.

After hitting the bulkhead for a few minutes, someone down the hall yelled out my name.

"Harris! You're down here!"

Somebody showed me how to make my rack, including two all-important details: You need twelve inches of sheet showing where your pillow goes and six inches of sheet turn tucked in. There's one way, and one way only, to fold your sheet over on your pillow.

By this point, I was pretty overwhelmed.

What in the world is happening to me?

Another plebe, Corey, had gone through the Naval Academy Prep School and was accustomed to these rituals. We met when he bolted through the door of my room, chopping, filling the small space with the spit-and-polished perfection of some poster boy Midshipmen. Next thing I knew he was schooling me on how to fold my clothes— "Make sure your socks have a little smiley face"—as the sound of various upperclassmen harassing other plebes echoed down the hall.

When the cadre left and we could relax a bit, Corey's demeanor immediately changed. The robotic military swagger vanished, and he turned into a regular guy.

I'll never forget what he told me.

"Just play the game, Mitch. Do what they say, but have fun with it. Just play the game."

This advice would come in handy.

***

My first morning in Bancroft was especially memorable.

Picture a hallway with old-timey tile, not only lining the floor but also extending all the way up the walls. That's the way Bancroft looks.

Around 5 a.m., one of the cadres went into one of the empty rooms and grabbed a small metallic towel rod. Then a bunch of them gathered at one end of the hall and flung this little torture device all the way to the other end. Then they threw it the other way. Back and forth. On and on it went. Six or seven or eight times...the rod bouncing off the tile, sliding and clanking on the floor...making the most incredible racket...until every plebe on the hall was awake.

That's how we were roused out of our racks that morning and every day that summer, like we were being bombarded by the enemy.

Sometimes I can hear that menacing noise in my nightmares.

As part of our morning routine, we were expected to rip off our sheets and line up in the hallway, holding the bed clothes in a certain manner straight out in front of your chest. No big deal, right? Well try holding a pillowcase full of sheets that way for a long time—maybe two, or three, or four minutes—while the cadres watch. They got pretty heavy, and you could see guys shaking and struggling to hold the linens in place.

"You guys are coming to the Academy, and you can't even hold up a bag of sheets?!"

This was yet another little test, and like all the others, you felt enormous pressure to measure up.

Eventually, the cadres ordered us to return to our rooms to make our beds within a short amount of time, and you couldn't possibly complete this chore without help. You needed a buddy to keep it tucked in on one side while you tucked it in on the other.

It didn't take us long to understand that the Academy designed this daily requirement with a deeper meaning: to teach the importance of teamwork—learning to count on other Midshipmen.

You didn't want to be the first one to finish because that just meant you would have to answer a bunch of random questions from the cadres. But you sure didn't want to be the last to hit the bulkhead.

Some plebes struggled, and when they didn't complete the assignment on time, the upperclassmen screamed in their faces at the top of their lungs. The tension mounted in those moments, and some couldn't handle the pressure.

After a while you start to learn: A big part of this whole experience was learning to handle—and thrive—under all sorts of pressure.

Periodic inspections were rigorous. Upperclassman would sweep a white glove across your rack and desk.

"Oh, here's a tiny hair on your desk. You fail!"

To keep you on your toes, they often sent someone to your room just before an impending inspection to ransack it. We called this the tornado treatment. Suddenly, you might find your alarm clock in the trash can or your toothbrush hidden deep beneath the covers in your roommate's rack.

This provoked yet another test, as the clock ticked.

"Being a plebe, life just sort of sucked," recalled my baseball teammate Mark McCoy. "It's the mental exhaustion of knowing: 'I've been doing this for four months, and I still have another three months to go...' Most of us were pretty cynical, Alpha-type guys who didn't like taking orders from other people...You don't understand why you're doing all this stuff...I don't think you really appreciate plebe year at the Academy till you graduate."

In time, all of us would come to appreciate the big picture and be thankful for the lessons we had learned in Annapolis, including McCoy, who would soon be leading men in Afghanistan.

Many aspects of the discipline around our rooms and elsewhere were designed to teach us attention to detail. In time, we all learned that in the fleet, attention to detail could save someone's life.

Every morning included calisthenics on the parade field, led by a guy on a platform and with various cadres patrolling for slackers.

"That's not a pushup!"

"Back to 1!"

"All the way down! All the way up!"

"Up! Down! Up! Down!"

We spent much of our time running in formation that summer, filling the air with the sound of one of our cadence songs, usually two or three miles at a time.

During Plebe Summer, we learned sailing techniques and took instruction in wrestling, mixed martial arts, boxing, and swimming. Someday you might have to flee a sinking ship, so everyone was carefully trained how to properly jump from a 10-meter board into a pool.

The Academy intricately choreographed meals at King Hall.

We lined up by company at a series of tables, each of us standing at attention in front of our designated seat.

The cadres attention to detail was ever present, and only when all was right would they say, "Seats!"

The noise of all of us sitting down in union sounded like a clap of thunder.

You didn't sit all the way back in your seat. Or at least you never did that twice. You sat at attention, at a 90-degree angle, with your eyes "in the boat." This was Navy slang for the thousand-yard stare, straight ahead.

While you were trying to eat at the proper 90-degree angle, staring into nothing, various upperclassmen wandered around, picking on the plebes. You tried to go unnoticed, hoping they wouldn't hound you for eating in the wrong position. You prayed that they would not call on you to answer some random question—perhaps about an item in the news, some Reef Points quote, or the amount of milk on the table—because a wrong answer could trigger some painful consequences.

Memorization is tough for me, and I struggled to commit the Reef Points and other facts to memory. Nerves may have made this situation even worse. I didn't want to mess up, and sometimes I pressed too hard. Some of the cadres made a special point of calling on me, and when they learned I was an athlete, some may have pushed me a little harder. Perhaps they wanted to make sure I deserved to be there, that I belonged and was willing, and able, to pay the price.

There was a stereotype about athletes, a belief among some of the other Midshipmen that maybe some of us had negotiated an easier road to the Academy, and certainly this was true in my case. I knew I was fortunate to be there and didn't want anybody to take it easy on me.

About a week into Plebe Summer, a couple of cadres stormed into my room.

"Pack your stuff! You're going home!"

I swallowed hard.

"You don't cut it here!"

A chill ran through my entire body.

What? What have I done?

"Sir, I don't understand..."

"You heard me! Pack your stuff! You're going home!"

Then they made it clear that this command also applied to my new roommate, who became pretty upset.

"We're gonna call your parents! You're both out of here tomorrow!"

I could feel my whole life—including my fledgling baseball career—slipping away, with no idea what I had done to deserve this fate.

I just knew that I had blown my big chance.

These two upperclassmen kept screaming at us, so we reluctantly gathered our belongings.

Then a memory washed over me.

"Just play the game, Mitch."

Corey had unwittingly prepared me for this moment as well as so many others.

It suddenly dawned on me that these two Midshipmen didn't have the power to kick us out of the Academy, so I started to breathe a little easier, even as they insisted we were toast.

Looking back on the situation now, I suspect those guys were testing us, to see how we would react. Would we curl up in a ball and start to cry? Would we beg? Would we fight to hold onto something that was precious to us?

No. We just kept playing the game.

No one was sent home, and those two upperclassmen learned that the baseball player from North Carolina wasn't looking for an easy way out.

***

In September 2024, I took my wife Mandi and our two children (seven-year-old daughter Rylan and six-year-old son Camden) on a tour of the Naval Academy. We were on campus for a baseball clinic.

It was a day of unavoidable emotion for me, especially when we reached the legendary Memorial Hall, located up a flight of stairs in Bancroft.

It was impossible for me to forget my first visit to this hallowed room two decades earlier.

Some events stick with you for a lifetime, and I still get choked up thinking about that foundational moment in my Academy experience.

On the first day of Plebe Summer, they convened us inside the large shrine, which had inspired Midshipmen since 1906. Standing there, you felt the history, the heroism, and the sacrifice seeping through the walls. A website devoted to the place described it this way:

> Memorial Hall...silently teaches the future leaders of the Naval Academy from the experiences of her fallen. She defines the fearless determination, the gallantry, the character of the officers that graduate from the halls of Bancroft...She enshrines within her walls the legacy of the everyday officers who three-hundred-sixty-five days a year put their safety, well-being, future, and dreams on the line with no questions asked for our freedom...She is a constant reminder the cost of freedom is immeasurable.

We learned about the founding of the U.S. Navy in 1775, several months before the thirteen original American colonies declared their independence, and how early figures including John Paul Jones, David

Farragut, Stephen Decatur, and George Dewey set the tone for a powerful and feared fighting force. We learned about the origins of the Naval Academy, why it was founded, and about epic battles led and won by Academy men, including the Battle of Leyte Gulf, the largest Naval engagement in modern history, which dealt a devastating blow to the Japanese during the desperate days of World War II.

Every night during Plebe Summer, we gathered in our main hallway to read the citation for a different Medal of Honor recipient. In those moments, the names etched in stone in Memorial Hall took on greater meaning for all of us.

Night after night, we learned in graphic detail about some former midshipman who had displayed unbelievable courage under incredibly difficult conditions, and in many cases, died in the process. We heard about the missions they accomplished during wars that our ancestors fought to preserve our republic.

Then we always closed by singing "Blue and Gold," the Academy alma mater:

> *Now colleges from sea to sea*
> *May sing of colors true*
> *But who has better right than we*
> *To hoist a symbol hue*
> *For sailors brave in battle fair*
> *Since fighting days of old*
> *Have proved the sailor's right to wear*
> *The Navy blue and gold*

This was always followed with a boisterous "Beat Army!"

Looking back on those solemn readings now, I remember thinking: *Do I have those kinds of qualities? Could I do those sorts of heroic things for these people standing beside me? How am I ever going to do anything to be worthy of the sacrifices made by the warriors remembered and studied and venerated in this room?*

The enormity of the place and what it represented started to sink in, and I began to fully appreciate the incredible opportunity I had been given.

I was still so young, still trying to figure out who I was and who I wanted to be.

Remember, only a few months before all this, I didn't really know anything about the Naval Academy.

Annapolis was a word without meaning to me.

And now?

Something was bubbling inside me—a force much stronger than a five-year legal commitment.

That first year in Annapolis, my baseball dream was stronger than ever, and I was determined to have a great college career.

I needed baseball, in ways I didn't fully understand.

But it turns out I needed something else too.

Gradually, as the Academy experience began to wash over me, as those moving Medal of Honor citations pulled me deeper and deeper into a world that had once seemed foreign to me, becoming a Naval officer and trying to measure up to this high standard became a new raging ambition, every bit as powerful as my desire to someday play baseball at the highest level.

Getting my commission and serving my country by leading sailors on the high seas was something I was now chasing with every fiber of my being.

Baseball and the Navy.

How could I know that my two dreams were on a collision course?

***

I lost about twenty pounds during Plebe Summer, and in one way at least, my daily workout got even more rigorous for the fall semester, as I moved up to the seventh floor. You haven't lived until you've chopped up and down seven flights.

My new roommate was Nathan Getty, and Ian Higgins joined us the next year. We would all stay together for the rest of our time at Annapolis. Getty was from Maryland, and his older brother had also attended the Academy, so he could share some insider knowledge. We all became great friends.

Fortunately, the cadres discontinued their summer alarm system, but this meant you were responsible for getting your own sorry butt out of bed. Furthermore, like other plebes, I had to get up early and station myself at a predetermined spot in the hallway, where I readied myself to recite the menu for the next three meals.

Sir, breakfast for today is...

These were known as Chow Calls.

Cadres also expected us to know an important piece of news and sports information for the day. The detailers approached their favorite targets and put them on the spot.

We were Siri before Siri.

The last thing you wanted to have to say was: "I'll find out, sir." This was a big failure, and the detailers remembered when you forgot or didn't know.

The harassment by the upperclassmen continued throughout plebe year, and some were tougher than others. But most of us understood the game by then. If you made it through Plebe Summer, you weren't going to quit, unless your grades were so bad they sent you home.

Adding classes to the mix presented a whole new level of pressure.

Growing up, I did well in school without having to study much. I quickly realized this wasn't going to work at the Academy.

Chemistry really kicked my butt that year, and I'll never forget being confronted with the first D of my life.

How in the world am I going to make it?

Around this time, it started to dawn on me that I really didn't know how to study. Reading a book didn't make a powerful impression on me. I needed to hear and see to learn, so I figured out how to be a better listener and note-taker in class. Eventually, moving into my engineering courses, carrying a heavy twenty-four-credit-hour load each semester, I found a new comfort zone. But I had to work my butt off to earn that degree.

As a freshman, you were stuck on campus. On Saturdays, you could leave the yard during the day but had to return that evening. On Sundays, you were allowed off during the day but must be back for formation prior to dinner. It could feel a little claustrophobic at times, so you learned to find creative ways to mentally escape the unrelenting pressure of the place.

On the secluded top floor of four-story Luce Hall, a small bunch of us—six or seven who were starting to form a tight, life-long bond—regularly snuck away to spend our free Sunday nights binge-watching "Band of Brothers," the recently produced HBO series about the drive to defeat Hitler during World War II.

Sometimes we brought snacks or a pizza from Steerage, a small grill located deep inside Bancroft—accessible only by midshipmen, faculty, and staff.

Watching the dramatized story about the famed Easy company, part of the U.S. Army's 101st Airborne Division, as they negotiated the treacherous journey from jump school to Normandy to V-E Day, it was impossible for us not to see glimpses into our own lives—and what might be.

Slightly more than three years after the 9/11 terrorist attacks, American forces were engaged in bloody wars in Iraq and Afghanistan. Military officers around our age fought and died every day, and we often received word about some Academy graduate who had recently perished in combat.

We didn't talk too much about the daily horrors of our own century, but on those memorable Sunday nights, when we began to feel like a band of brothers, we soaked up the powerful history lesson with increasingly sober eyes.

***

On the last day of every plebe year, the various companies compete against each other in a two-day event called Sea Trials. This includes running a 5-mile race in boots, running through an obstacle course, doing team sit-ups with a telephone poll, push-ups, and the Herndon Monument climb.

The iconic 21-foot-high stone monument, which sits just outside the campus chapel, was erected in honor of Commander William Lewis Herndon, who went down with a ship during a hurricane off the coast of North Carolina in 1857, after "a gallant effort to save it, its sailors and passengers."

The traditional climax of the plebe year, which dates back to 1962, was memorable for all of us, as we worked together to mount an assault on the stone obelisk, lathered with vegetable shortening and, therefore, incredibly slippery. Just for the occasion, a plebe cover had been placed atop the marker, and the object was to build a human ladder to the top, so one of us could snag the cap and replace it with an officer's cover.

This took strategy and teamwork. After all, the offensive lineman for the football team isn't going to climb on some little woman's shoulders. When one of us started to slip and slide, we had to pull him or her back from the edge and keep climbing. But we figured it out in good time, and when one of us reached up there and made the switch, we all cheered.

Plebe year was over.

Officially we were now third-class Midshipmen.

We could all walk a little taller now.

***

I was happy to be playing Division I baseball. Honestly, I was just happy to still be playing the game I loved. But none of us had any illusions about Navy's place in the greater scheme of collegiate baseball.

The Patriot League, with rivals including Bucknell, Lehigh, and Holy Cross, held tight to the bottom rung of Division I, and we were constantly confronted with the reality that very few people cared about Navy baseball.

The old wooden bleachers that had so shocked Mom and Dad on our recruiting trip the previous spring were practically empty for every home game. A few parents showed up, but players could hear spectator conversations while standing on first base.

The coaches used me as utility infielder, at first and third, and worked me into the rotation in the bullpen. I pitched a total of fifteen innings my freshman season in 2005, and we struggled.

At the end of the 12-33-1 season, head coach Steve Whitmyer was relieved of his baseball duties and reassigned.

I didn't know then what this meant for my future.

4
Something to Prove

WHENEVER I RETURNED HOME to see my folks, Dad and I usually wound up in the yard. Catch remained part of the fabric of our close relationship. It was still a fun thing to do, a father and a son clinging to a timeless ritual overflowing with a certain unmistakable nostalgia.

We had some great conversations throwing the ball back and forth, reinforcing our strong bond.

Dad encouraged me to throw it as hard as I could, and as my arm kept getting stronger and stronger, he sometimes struggled to catch the ball.

Hate to admit it, but those times when my fastball caught him in the palm, I tried to hide my proud grin.

But early during my Naval Academy career, not long after Dad took a new job and they moved to a nearby town in Maryland, he waved me off.

"Can't catch you anymore, son," he said. "Your ball's just too hard and fast. It's on me before I know it. I'd like to keep my teeth."

This was sort of a sad moment in our relationship, the end of something, but it also reflected an inflection point in my athletic career.

Returning to campus for my sophomore year was surreal.

The first time I entered Bancroft, it felt strange to walk along the wall. I was waiting for someone to tell me to get my knees up.

The plebe experience is so overwhelming, it completely takes over your thought process. You start to see all these rules dictating every aspect of your behavior, especially toward the all-powerful upperclassmen.

Then you become a sophomore, and you walk back into the same environment, and believe me, it takes time to adjust to a new level of freedom while dealing with the same all-consuming pressures to meet the various high standards of Academy life.

It's great to be a sophomore, but it can take a while to get the plebe out of your head.

My second year of Navy baseball was equally jarring.

Coach Whitmyer's reassignment to another job on campus turned out to be a lucky break for me. He would spend the rest of his career doing good things for the Academy, but baseball needed new leadership.

Determined to upgrade the program, Navy hired Paul Kostacopoulos, who had built winning programs at Providence and Maine. He was very knowledgeable about the game and detail-oriented. The commitment to upgrade our facilities—including replacing the old wooden bleachers at Max Bishop Stadium with a modern-looking permanent structure with 1,500 seats and remodeling our outdated locker room—struck a more positive tone for the future, especially after the gloom of five straight losing seasons.

Soon after, we returned in the fall of 2005, the new head coach convened a team meeting in the bleachers overlooking the field. Not knowing what to expect, we all sat nervously as he looked up at us from the grass and jolted us out of our complacency.

"Here's the deal," he said, looking around at the faces of the men he had inherited, "if you think you have a position, you don't."

No one said a word.

No one knew where this was heading.

Because the Academy doesn't offer athletic scholarships, no athlete could be run off by a coach, but the new man was taking charge and figuring out how to exploit his available leverage.

"What we're gonna do is basically have open tryouts. By the end of the fall, we'll have a team. If you make it, you make it. If you don't, you don't."

A jolt of nervous energy surged through the team because we could all tell this coach meant business. He wanted to win, and he challenged us to meet a higher standard or make room for somebody who actually wanted to play.

I wasn't rattled by this gauntlet that had just been dropped at our feet. Not at all. Actually, this sort of competitive pressure was a powerful trigger for me, and suddenly, I was all fired up, determined to earn a place on the team.

The need to prove myself had been part of my motivational launch sequence from my earliest days in youth sports, and it would remain a central component in my unlikely journey to the front pages of sports sections across the country in the years ahead. This tapped into something deep down into who I was and why I played the game. If we were competing, I desperately wanted to beat you, and if you doubted me, I wanted to prove you wrong.

Now I needed to show this coach what I could do.

***

The weight that had fallen off so easily during Plebe Summer eventually went back on, and fall baseball workouts helped me build muscle and strength. My body was maturing. Standing 6-foot-4 and weighing 215 pounds, I was one of the biggest guys on the team, with no more than 9 percent body fat.

The coaches weren't sure where they wanted to use me, but I wound up working with the pitchers in a rotating bullpen during fall camp. Coach Kostacopoulos and pitching coach Scott Friedholm carefully studied all of us, and when my time came, I performed well. Clearly, they liked what they were seeing.

Friedholm started peppering me with questions about my background and eventually got around to the subject of my rather disappointing freshman year.

"How did your season go last year?"

"Well, I only threw fifteen innings."

"Really?"

He seemed surprised that the previous staff had not used me more as a pitcher.

Mark McCoy had been the number-one starter the previous year, the one stud on a rather mediocre staff, and remembered me as "a skinny guy" whose mechanics "weren't all that good."

"Sophomore fall, it was like Mitch all the sudden came back a man," he said.

After McCoy first noticed that my arm was getting stronger, he encouraged the new coaching staff to look at using me as a starting pitcher. "Mitch's fastball kept getting faster and faster as we moved through the fall," McCoy said.

Eventually, Friedholm got around to telling me that the radar guns showed I was hitting as high as 90 miles per hour in the bullpen.

"What? Really?"

This came as a complete shock.

"You mean this isn't what you normally do?" Friedholm asked.

Shaking my head, I explained that the highest I had ever clocked was the mid-80s.

I was definitely feeling stronger in my delivery but this was a brand new digital neighborhood for my arm.

Curious to see my full capability, he took a few minutes to show me how to grip and throw a cut fastball.

Lucky me, on the very first try, I threw the ball toward the plate, and it cut right to left, about two inches. Perfect. Just what you want—that last late bite.

Friedholm stood just behind me, and I could hear him cackling. "Do that again!"

I had never thrown a cutter before in my life and didn't know why he was laughing. It was a little distracting.

After throwing another cutter, I could tell the catcher was having a hard time handling my ball.

"Throw another fastball," said the voice from behind.

Whoosh. Just right.

"Now go back to the cutter."

I wound up and let it go.

By the time this one landed right on the mark, my new coach was practically giddy as he told me he had seen enough.

"You're probably going to be our number-one guy," he said loud enough for several other pitchers to hear.

I just looked at him for a moment, in utter disbelief.

***

Over the next several months, Friedholm coached me to become a better pitcher. He could see I had great potential but still had a long way to go, especially in adding a measure of finesse to my growing power.

After rearranging various parts, Coach Kostacopoulos put a very competitive team on the field in 2006. Our 32-21-1 record represented a significant step forward for Navy baseball, and it was a breakout year for me as one of four starting pitchers.

"Every outing, Mitch got better," McCoy said. "He just made adjustments so quickly, and his ability just sort of took over."

With my velocity continuing to improve—consistently clocking in the low-90s—I finished 10-3 with a 1.74 ERA, which earned me Patriot League Pitcher of the Year. My 113 strikeouts set a new conference record.

Starting out, I was all talent and very little strategy—mostly focused on using my power to get the ball from the mound to the plate. McCoy helped me understand the art of pitching. He had developed so many tools in the competitive high school environment of South Florida, and he generously taught me how to be a smarter pitcher. I'll always be grateful for his help and friendship, even as we competed with each other.

"Mitch was still working to refine his cutter...it took some time for him to perfect that pitch," McCoy said. "Once he did that, he was pretty much unhittable."

One day, Mom and Dad were sitting in the virtually empty stands when I was pitching, and they noticed a stranger walk up, take a seat, and start taking notes.

"You have to understand: the crowds were so small—that day, maybe fifteen people—that we were almost on a first-name basis with everybody," Dad said.

As one of my fastballs blew past the batter, the stranger yelled out, loud enough for all to hear, "Holy crap!"

A few moments later, I launched another rocket and the man was clearly impressed.

Leaning toward some nearby folks, he said, "Who's this pitching?"

Pointing a few rows away, the man said, "Well, that's his parents right there!"

"That's your son?"

"Yeah."

"Where's he been?"

Dad laughed.

It turned out that the man was a scout for the New York Yankees, on his way home from a trip to see some hot prospect. He had just stopped at our isolated little baseball outpost on a lark. But he would be back, and in time, there would be others.

In my last start of the year, a 2-0 victory over Coppin State, I threw a complete game no-hitter—only the fifth in 111 years of Navy baseball.

On days when I didn't pitch, I frequently made the lineup at first base or designated hitter. During one stretch, I hit safely in eleven consecutive games.

"Mitch is simply an excellent baseball player," Kostacopoulos told Navy Sports. "He's an outstanding Midshipman and a fine young man."

But my year and perhaps my entire future turned on one unlikely play at the plate.

Toward the middle of the season, we were playing on the road at University of Maryland Baltimore County. Standing on third base as a DH, after reaching with a base hit, I watched as one of my teammates hit a fly ball into left field. It wasn't very deep but deep enough, so after the left fielder made the catch, I tagged and headed for home.

Now, I wasn't very fast. But I wasn't exactly a slug for a guy my size, and I believed I could beat the throw.

When I was maybe 10 feet from home plate, barreling toward that precious run, the catcher took one step up the third-base line. Forced to adjust, I slid toward home, kicking him pretty hard down low, colliding with him, and sliding all the way to the plate, where the umpire called me safe.

With my body sprawled over and adjacent to the plate, my world suddenly shifted into slow motion.

The first thing I remember is a jolt of excruciating pain.

Then I looked down to see the bottom of my left cleat, with my ankle pointed away from my leg at a 90-degree angle. It was a nasty sight. That's when they thought I went into shock. The trauma was too much for me to process as a crowd started to form around my battered body. It all started to feel like a weird dream.

Loren "Ship" Shipley, our veteran trainer, raced out of the visitors' dugout and to the scene.

I was glad to see him, but by this time, was freaking out.

"Ship! Look at my ankle!"

Two of the coaches moved in to hold me down because they didn't know how bad it was and didn't want me to make it worse by trying to get up.

Quickly assessing the situation, Ship could see that my ankle was dislocated, not broken, so he made a fateful decision: After handing me a towel to bite down on for the pain about to shoot through my body, he carefully popped the bone back into place.

Looking back, I feel incredibly lucky that I had a wily professional with such a deft touch on the scene at this pivotal moment in my career.

Some of the guys helped me up and over to the dugout, and I sat there for the rest of the game, nursing the injury with ice and Ibuprofen.

Once we got back to campus, they put me in a boot, and I worried that my season could be over, that I might be looking at surgery or lengthy rehabilitation. My ankle had swollen and it was very painful.

The next morning, the team doctor was dumbfounded. Looking at the X-ray, he confirmed that there was no bone break, no hairline fracture, no tendon tear, no ligament tear, only a high-ankle sprain.

Of course, several people had seen the dislocation up close, and the doctor could not explain how Ship could have popped it back into place without any lingering evidence of significant trauma.

Ship sat there with me in the doctor's office, and he just started laughing. "Never in my life have I seen anything like this!"

Breathing a huge sigh of relief, I turned my attention to two upcoming Army-Navy games at Baltimore's Camden Yards, home of the Orioles. No way I wanted to miss the biggest showdown of our year, not if I could walk.

Ultimately, this would be a decision for Ship and the coaches, but I started lobbying my trainer on the way out of the doctor's office, even as I hobbled down the hallway on crutches.

"Eleven days. What do you think?"

Ship admired my spunk but looked at me with an exasperated expression. "Mitch, you've just dislocated your ankle..."

I didn't want to do anything foolish, but all of a sudden, I had a little something to prove.

***

For the next eleven days, I practically lived in the training room. This included hours and hours in the whirlpool and a treatment called "milking": While lying face-down on a table with my bad foot in the air, Ship lathered my ankle in lotion and started pushing the blood out—squeezing the area like crazy. We did that several times a day, and it hurt like hell. To get my muscles moving again, I would pick up marbles with my toes and do this exercise where I sketched out the entire alphabet with my foot. Over and over again. Some of this I did while studying, because there were only so many hours in a day, and I couldn't afford to fall behind on my classes.

An overriding thought pounded in my head: *Missing the opportunity to play for the first time in a Major League stadium is not an option.*

Fortunately, this injury was to my landing foot. If it had happened instead to my right foot? No way I would have made it back so quickly.

Six days before the Army doubleheader, my boot was off for good. I couldn't run, but I walked just fine, so after pleading my case to the coaches, they allowed me to throw a bullpen and video tape it, to compare to my normal body movement. When I passed this test—going through my usual mechanics and clocking in with one 94-mph fastball—the staff gave the go-ahead for me to get ready to start the first game against the hated Black Knights.

Walking into Camden Yards, soaking up the incredible atmosphere in downtown Baltimore, I couldn't help but think about all the history. In my mind, I could picture the legendary Cal Ripken, Jr. scooping up a ground ball and throwing to first. It was like walking into a shrine, and so special that I was getting a chance to play on that field with my buddies.

Time in the training room cut into my regular pre-game routine. We treated my ankle, still swelling, with both hot and cold baths. We carefully taped it and encased it in a special brace, so bulky that I struggled to lace up my cleat. No one could say what might happen if I had to lunge suddenly for a hot ground ball, but I was raring to go.

Whether I would actually be ready was a game-time decision, and some of our guys—who had seen my ankle turned sideways just eleven days before—were surprised when I stepped on the mound. Looking out into the announced crowd of 2,500 fans, by far the biggest audience of my life, I felt grateful to Ship and the coaches for helping me recover enough to make it back in time.

"It was pretty scary what happened to Mitchell, but how he came back...it was something special to see," said my mom, who joined my dad in the stands.

I pitched well, scattering six hits across six innings, but we wound up losing, 4-0. However, we beat Army, 2-0, in the second game, thanks to a gem by McCoy.

My personal victory didn't show up on the scoreboard, but those eleven days marked me.

I proved something to my coaches and teammates, and to myself.

***

Some of the best stories about the game of baseball never really happened.

Robert Redford's Roy Hobbs never played for the long-suffering, fictional New York Knights. But the 1984 film *The Natural* reminds us how a middle-aged man beaten down by life, haunted by his past, can follow his heart to his own happy ending.

If you aren't rooting for him to choose the right girl and be there at the end to help his team win the pennant, you don't have a heart.

The mythology of baseball is one of its enduring charms. Sometimes, it tells us who we are, if we're willing to listen.

In 1985, celebrated writer George Plimpton's *Sports Illustrated* story about Sidd Finch, a pitching prospect for the New York Mets, captured the country's imagination. Could this unknown phenom raised in an English orphanage really throw a 168-mph fastball? It all seemed too good to be true, and of course it was. Finch was a multi-layered figment of Plimpton's fertile imagination, an elaborate April Fool's joke.

Growing up around the game, I learned that at any given time, a relatively small number of pitchers across the country could throw in the mid-90s and beyond, and that most of those were either in the big leagues, or in the pipeline trying to get to the big leagues.

It takes many things for a pitcher to make it at the highest level, many things that the radar guns can't measure, but I knew that if I could ever get my velocity up to that area, I would get some looks.

The first time I saw Dennis Quaid's portrayal of former Tampa Bay Devil Rays pitcher Jim Morris in 2002's *The Rookie*, it was through the eyes of a high school athlete who thought it was cool that a thirty-five-year-old high school coach could make the most of an unlikely second chance—riding his once-battered but reinvigorated arm all the way to the Major Leagues.

You want to cheer for an "old man" science teacher who keeps the scouts waiting while he changes a dirty diaper—and then strokes twelve consecutive 98-mph fastballs.

Never did I imagine that I would actually get to know the real Morris, or that I would one day lean on his incredible tale as proof of something—when I was desperately trying to hold on to my own dream.

But I'm getting a little ahead of the story.

You need to hear about a defining moment during my junior year at the Academy.

Several days into fall practice in 2006, we were preparing for our first scrimmage game. It was early afternoon when I walked over from the main part of campus to our stadium, located right across College Creek, and I noticed a big crowd of cars and trucks, which was odd. We didn't get big crowds for our real games in the spring, much less for an intersquad game in the fall.

Seeing Coach Kostacopoulos, I walked up to him with a puzzled expression. "What's happening?"

He smiled. "You had a good year last year. They're here to see you!"

Scouts from many different Major League clubs had shown up, all armed with radar guns, which clocked me consistently in the mid-90s.

This is when my dream started to feel real.

In that moment, maybe I felt just a little of the emotion that had once bubbled up inside Jim Morris when he learned that all those scouts were drooling over him.

But he had his complications and I had mine.

***

At the end of my sophomore year, I had joined my whole company inside the solemn Memorial Hall as an officer led us through the signing of our so-called 2-for-7 contract.

He told us about what a big deal this was and made sure that we understood that, by signing, we effectively codified not only our commitment to our final two years at the Academy but also our five-year post-graduate commitment to the Navy. The contract further stipulated that if I decided to leave the Academy prior to the end of my fourth year, I would reimburse the government for the cost of my education.

This re-commitment step is the Navy's way of giving you one last chance to change your mind on the way to active duty, and some midshipmen take the final exit ramp.

If you don't sign it, you can leave the Academy without any repercussions.

This was a huge deal in my life, and the choice weighed on me, given my special circumstances.

No one could say if the Navy would allow me to play professional baseball.

I wasn't eligible to be drafted until after my junior year, so I had to make the 2-for-7 decision without truly understanding my options.

Somewhere I have a picture one of my classmates snapped of me, sitting on a bench, reading through the multi-page document, contemplating the consequences of my signature.

No one put a gun to my head. I was eager to have a career as a Naval officer, eager to serve my country.

But did this mean I had to give up my life-long dream to play professional baseball?

Couldn't we figure out a way for me to do both?

During this period, Kostacopoulos told a reporter about me: "He's very appreciative of what's been offered to him...That's why people are pulling for him. He's so appreciative."

Even before signing the 2-for-7, even before the scouts started descending on Max Bishop Stadium, I had sought the counsel of Coach Kostacopoulos and our athletic director, Chet Gladchuk, Jr.

What if...?

"We just don't know, Mitch," was the best they could offer.

I discussed the situation at length with my parents, and we all prayed about it.

Ultimately, I signed the 2-for-7, hoping that, if I was drafted, the Navy would treat me the same way it had treated other high-achieving athletes.

One well-known example was basketball star David Robinson, who led the underdog Midshipmen to the NCAA East Regional finals in 1986, the year before he won the Naismith Award as national player-of-the-year. Robinson was a beast, and he became a great ambassador for the Navy. The San Antonio Spurs selected the center first overall in the 1987 NBA draft, with the understanding that he could not play immediately. After serving two years in the Reserves, the Navy allowed him to start his professional basketball career, becoming one of the biggest stars in the NBA and leading the Spurs to two league championships.

Around the same time, the Navy also played ball with football star Napoleon McCallum. After graduating from the Academy in 1985 and spending time as a recruiting officer, he was assigned to a ship based in Long Beach as a supply officer, which allowed him to play the 1986 season with the Los Angeles Raiders. Publicity concerning the special arrangement may have played a role in his reassignment, which curtailed his playing career for the next three years, until he completed his five-year Navy commitment.

During my undergraduate years, the Department of Defense started giving the branches the latitude to approve early releases in exchange for longer reserve commitments.

West Point's policy was pragmatic and struck me as reasonable. They started allowing graduating cadet athletes with the opportunity to play professional sports to apply for admission to the so-called

Alternative Service Option, a program which enabled assignments to geographically favorable recruiting stations for two years. Then they could "buy out" the remaining three years of their active-duty commitment—by agreeing to serve six years in the U.S. Army Reserves.

Certainly, there are examples of athletes at Navy and the other service academies who fulfilled their full five-year commitment and then played professional sports, including Pro Football Hall of Famer Roger Staubach. After leading Navy to one of its best football seasons ever and winning the Heisman Trophy in 1963, Roger the Dodger was selected in the futures draft by the NFL's Dallas Cowboys. Staubach then served five years in the Navy, including a tour of duty in the Vietnam War. He was twenty-seven when he joined the Cowboys, and many assumed his best days were long gone. But he proved the skeptics wrong. Over the next decade, he led Dallas to four Super Bowls and became one of the greatest quarterbacks of all time.

What it must have taken for this steely competitor to return to the football field after five years away from the action.

Five years can be an eternity.

***

Despite nagging injuries, I had another good year as a junior, fashioning an 8-5 record with a 2.14 ERA and 119 strikeouts, breaking my own Patriot League record. Plus, I was a force on offense, leading the team in RBI (47) while hitting a solid .293. Being named a *Baseball America* Third-Team All-American was a big honor.

The scouts continued to show up, well aware that my ability to play professionally remained uncertain.

"Mitch had a very good arm," later recalled Koby Perez, who scouted the Middle Atlantic region for the St. Louis Cardinals. "He was a super athletic competitor who went about his business the right way."

In June 2007, when the Atlanta Braves drafted me in the 24th round, with the 738th overall pick, a dream of mine came true. I was the first Naval Academy junior ever drafted.

This was an incredible milestone, just three years after no other Division I program had been willing to sign me.

But it was also a frustrating time.

How was I supposed to feel?

To know that I was good enough to get a shot without knowing whether I would be allowed to accept this opportunity?

The Braves' decision to draft me—just in case something happened to make me available—would last for a full year.

I tried to put the situation out of my mind as I kept competing in Annapolis and beyond.

Playing in the Cape Cod League that summer allowed me to compete alongside a bunch of guys who would end up in the Major Leagues.

It also brought my peculiar dilemma into the spotlight.

The media attention was inevitable, and I dealt with it candidly.

"I was surprised at how early [I was drafted]," I told a reporter for the Cape Cod Times. "If [the Braves] did anything, I thought it would be much later, considering I told them there was no chance of me signing."

Striking a hopeful tone, I told the same reporter, "[The Navy doesn't] want to take away the possibility of me playing ball. They're trying to figure out a way I can play ball and fulfill my commitment."

***

Between my junior and senior years, I met or spoke with every single Major League team.

Interest in me was high, as I was ranked among the top senior pitching prospects in the country by several different sources.

After every meeting, I collected the representative's business card, and soon pinned them above the desk in my dorm room—a constant reminder of my quest, even as it became incredibly elusive.

This little ritual reinforced a message pounding in my head: *You're wanted, and you can do it. It's as close as one of those business cards. But it's going to be more difficult than you had imagined. You're going to have to fight even harder for your dream.*

Usually when a prospect meets with club scouts and other officials, they are trying to evaluate your skills, personality, and character, so they can measure all those intangibles beyond the reach of the radar gun. Before they waste a draft pick and invest the corresponding amount of money on you, they want to see if you are a solid citizen, how competitive you are, and if you are coachable.

But my situation was way more complicated.

They always wanted to know what it would take to convince the Navy to allow me to play.

What sort of deal could we make?

More than one wondered if the Navy would allow me to play immediately after graduation and start my active duty after the season.

Also discussed was the previously approved Pentagon policy that essentially would have had me serve a two-year active-duty commitment and then be able to play baseball with another extended commitment—perhaps three or more years—in the Navy Reserves.

Attacking the situation from another angle, I suggested that if I was allowed to sign with a club that paid me a significant bonus, I could then turn around and reimburse the government for the cost of my education and immediately play.

"We talked about that a lot," Mom said. "What if a club wants him and is willing to pay the government back? Would they let him graduate and just not be commissioned?"

I had all the time in the world to fulfill my duties as a Naval officer, but with each passing year, my baseball skills would diminish.

What can we do? How can we make it work?

Various scenarios were floated, but before and during my senior season, when I continually clocked a 95-mph fastball, I couldn't offer any real guidance to the teams that considered drafting me because, officially at least, the Navy had slammed the door.

In a memorandum dated November 2, 2007, Donald C. Winter, the Secretary of the Navy, stated:

> ...When the nation is not at war, exceptional personnel with unique talents and abilities may be released from active duty when there is a strong expectation that they will provide the Navy and Marine Corps with significant favorable media exposure likely to enhance national recruiting or public affairs efforts. Personnel will be expected to use their talents in a manner that generates interest for service in the United States Navy and Marine Corps...
>
> However, as the Nation is at war and the other services have utilized Stop Loss authority to maintain readiness, I believe it is inappropriate to continue this policy. Accordingly, all submissions in accordance with this policy memorandum shall be held in abeyance until further notice.

Effectively, the Navy decided to start enforcing a higher standard just as the possibility of achieving my baseball dream started to materialize.

It also didn't help that a recent Academy football star, who had made some sort of deal to play for an NFL team, ran afoul of the Navy brass, poisoning the well for me.

***

Graduating from the Naval Academy on May 23, 2008 was one incredible moment.

Standing on the field at Navy-Marine Corps Memorial Stadium on a beautiful day in my dress whites, I tossed my cover into the air and then watched the Blue Angels roar overhead.

My parents, lost somewhere in the massive crowd, beamed with pride.

Trust me: There were plenty of days during my four years at the Academy when I thought that day would never come.

To finally reach the end and feel the achievement—and the burden lifted off my shoulders—was amazing.

I had worked my butt off to earn one of the most prestigious degrees in the world, and nobody could ever take that away from me.

Even amid the celebration with so many of my buddies, the irony of the situation wasn't lost on me. Baseball had brought me to Annapolis and made possible this first-class, life-altering education.

But how does my situation look now? Does having the diploma change anything about baseball?

About two weeks later, while on post-graduation leave, I visited my parents' house in Maryland, where Dad and I spent much of the morning monitoring the second day of the free agent draft on MLB Network.

Dad could see my agitation, wondering whether I would be drafted at all, and if so, how high?

"Why don't we get out of here and go play golf?"

Sounded like a good idea to me.

A few hours later, we approached the turn on a nearby golf course when my cell phone rang. It was my agent.

"Hey, Mitch, congratulations! You just went in the 13th round to the St. Louis Cardinals."

The Cardinals selected me 395th overall, which represented a sizable gamble under the circumstances. But according to others, I could have gone much higher.

"The Navy situation affected Mitch's draft position tremendously," said the Cardinals' Perez. "If he had been at a normal school, say the University of Maryland instead of Annapolis, he probably would have been a third- or fourth-round talent. But people weren't going to risk that high of a pick, not knowing whether he could sign or not."

Finding an ally in former Naval aviator John Abbamondi, who served as Assistant General Manager for the Cardinals and was hopeful that a solution could be found, Perez lobbied on my behalf with other decision-makers in the front office. "I think we should take a flyer on him," he argued. "In case he's able to ever come out, we can have the rights to him."

When I was still available in the 13th round, "it became a risk worth taking."

Of course, it was a tremendous thrill to be drafted for the second time, but it was hard to get very excited, especially because the 13th round didn't do anything to move the needle for the Navy. It didn't make me look like a sure thing.

There was a heavy weight to the day. My dream was fulfilled—but not really. Did it mean something big or nothing at all? Who knew?

Meanwhile, the Navy allowed one of my teammates to leave and sign a good contract without any sort of penalty.

Oliver Drake was a year behind me and a good pitching prospect.

Because he had attended prep school before enrolling at the Academy and reached his twenty-first birthday during his sophomore year, he was eligible for the draft in 2008 and selected by the Orioles in the 43rd round. Influenced by the uncertainty of my situation, he left the Academy before signing the 2-for-7, leaving him with no Navy commitment to fulfill. He signed with Baltimore and would spend the next six years slogging through the Orioles' minor league system before finally making his Major League debut in 2015—a month after mine. He wound up playing for seven different teams.

With my frustration building, I quietly considered my options.

I didn't want to sue the Navy.

I didn't want to go public about my situation.

Honestly, I didn't want to do anything to give the Navy a black eye.

What could I do?

Privately, I met with an attorney in the Navy's Judge Advocate General division, in an effort to understand the early release policy and how we might figure out a workable solution.

"Help me," I said, "because I don't get it."

I told her I would do whatever the Navy asked of me, including turning myself into a walking, talking recruiting poster for the Navy and the Academy. Could no one understand the publicity goldmine this represented—especially at a time of war?

"I'll wear my uniform to and from games," I pleaded. "I'll mention the Navy and the Naval Academy in every interview."

The JAG lawyer listened to me and seemed to appreciate my dilemma and my desire to do the right thing.

After examining the policy, she said the Navy had the power to make me serve four years as an enlisted man and reimburse the government for the cost of my education—if they thought I was trying to get out of my commission.

She then offered some blunt advice.

"Don't be the poster child for them. They will throw the book at you and make an example of you."

5

The Scenic Route

IN A WAR ZONE, especially in the age of asymmetric threats, you can measure the line between belligerence and tactical retreat in feet and seconds.

Danger is often a judgment call.

This I know from personal experience.

Many of my Academy classmates saw brutal combat in Iraq and Afghanistan. I was lucky. I didn't have people shooting at me every day.

But during a six-month deployment to the Persian Gulf in 2009, I repeatedly looked into the face of enemy combatants who delighted in harassing the United States Navy, often pushing us to the edge of that fine line.

Fortunately, I had been well-prepared to man a post on the high seas during my four years at the Academy.

Not long after graduation in June 2008, I was assigned as the weapons officer on the USS Ponce, a small Austin-class amphibious transport ship.

For several months, the Ponce (LPD-15) was docked in the shipyard adjacent to the massive Naval Station Norfolk on Virginia's Atlantic coast, which would become my permanent home base throughout my Navy career. The 16,000-ton ship, launched in 1970, measured 570 feet long and could accommodate twenty-nine officers and 487 crew. By Navy standards, the Ponce was old. It was approaching the end of its operational life. When I arrived, the Ponce was in the middle of a whole-scale upgrade to prepare for its latest mission.

Our aft landing deck was big enough to accommodate an MV-22 Osprey, and it was incredible to see that remarkable Marine aircraft take off and land vertically.

Eventually we steamed toward the Gulf, bolstered by the addition of the 22nd Marine Expeditionary Unit (known as "22 Meu").

Especially while navigating the Strait of Hormuz, the all-important, 90-mile-long passage that connects the Gulf of Oman and the Persian Gulf—through which about 25 percent of the world's oil flows—we often encountered suspicious vessels.

"Small boat, inbound" was an alert that immediately heightened tensions across the ship.

"Small" means nimble, in a way that our ship wasn't, and "small" could mean trouble.

As the weapons officer, I manned the radio, ready to order my people to fire on a threat if the captain escalated to what we called Condition 1.

Many times, the small boats would speed toward us, knowing we would have to interpret such behavior as the prelude to hostile action—pushing right up to the edge of an international incident before veering off at the last possible moment. It had become a familiar, and dangerous, routine.

Captain Tim Crone trained me to deal with such threats and understand our very strict rules of engagement for Operation Iraqi Freedom.

Our mission was to protect the shipping lanes and deter any hostile enemy from causing trouble around the oil platforms.

It was a place where terrorism and piracy were a daily fact of life.

One day on my watch, a small craft motored right up next to us, close enough for me to look directly into the eyes of a man wearing some sort of uniform, standing next to a .50-caliber gun, with an automatic rifle strapped across his shoulder. There was no flag, nothing to identify nationality, but the man, who appeared in charge, shouted something in Arabic. He was not happy.

Equipped with eight .50-caliber guns as well as the Phalanx CIWS weapons system, we were fully capable of blowing the boat out of the water, and I was going to protect my crew.

***

Some of my favorite times at the Naval Academy happened during our summer sea tours.

While serving on Navy ships alongside other midshipmen, and under the supervision of officers and enlisted sailors, I got to experience various aspects of life on the high seas, while learning specific jobs that would eventually inform my career as a surface warfare officer.

Navigation.

Propulsion.

Communications.

Our various training blocks proved eye-opening. Suddenly, it all started to get very real: As soon as I graduated, my primary home for a good portion of time would be on a ship.

One of the most memorable experiences was sailing with a group of eight midshipmen on a two-week exercise just off the Atlantic Coast. We started out at the Naval Academy Preparatory School in Newport, Rhode Island, and eventually navigated the 25-foot craft back through the Chesapeake Bay to the Academy.

What a learning experience, on various levels.

By the time I reported for my first active-duty deployment on the Ponce two years later, I was starting to get my sea legs.

Early in our deployment, we had a close call down deep in the bowels of the ship.

Few things are more dangerous on a ship than a bad boiler. When one of those steam generators explodes, the pressure can kill every nearby sailor and cause incredible damage capable of ripping through the ship.

We had this master chief who was a wily old veteran, and one day in the engineering room, he heard something that didn't sound quite right. The noise of the boiler sounded only faintly different, but he was attuned to this nuance. Acting quickly, he got everyone out of the boiler room, shut the boiler down, and inspected it—revealing a tiny crack.

The boiler could have blown at any time.

Later, this situation became a learning experience for me. I got up close and saw the inner workings of the massive boiler, including the tiny little hairline crack that could have caused a calamity.

"This is what kills people," one of the old hands said.

No doubt, the master chief saved many lives that day.

On our way to the Middle East, we stopped at several ports in the Mediterranean, including Italy, Greece, and Cypress and had a blast. Later, we ported in Jordan and Bahrain. It was eye-opening to see different cultures.

After dropping off the Marines in Kuwait, where they trained for oil platform defense, we returned to patrol the Gulf. The heat there often soared past 105 degrees Fahrenheit.

At times, it was incredibly peaceful out there, with the wind in your face and nothing around for miles and miles but clear blue water.

Often on Saturdays, we relaxed by grilling burgers on the flight deck. We had a hoop for basketball and a big net to catch golf balls. Some guys liked to fish off the back of the ship.

You get to know people when you live in such close quarters for six months at a time, and I made some great, life-long friends during that first deployment.

But we were living in a world forever changed by the terrorist attacks of September 11, 2001.

Danger lurked all around us.

By this time, the homeland was increasingly war weary, our military stretched thin.

Our vast military machine often struggled to defend against crude little bombs, known as improvised explosive devices (IEDs), which inflicted a steady drumbeat of casualties across two very different fronts.

The war in Afghanistan was approaching the eight-year mark. No longer was the country a safe haven for the Taliban and other terrorists who might attack the U.S., but the American military was still paying a huge price for holding territory and trying to build western-style civilian institutions, including free elections.

Every body bag shipped back to the states was a victory for the Taliban, determined to outlast us. They ultimately did.

Six years after the invasion of Iraq, which toppled the regime of Saddam Hussein, a bloody insurgency had inflicted more than 4,000 U.S. casualties. But by the time the Ponce arrived in the Gulf, the uprising had largely been defeated by an American troop escalation known as The Surge.

The insurgents and their allies on the high seas were battered, desperate and eager to grab any excuse to kill Americans.

A stray little boat with hostile intent could be the maritime equivalent of an IED.

That day on the bridge, with the little boat pulling right up to us, I walked that fine line, eyeball to eyeball with a potential enemy.

Unless they crossed the line into direct provocation—like firing a round from that .50 caliber—my hands were tied. If the shooting started, we all understood it would lead toward a place loaded with unpredictable consequences, as the U.S. began to withdraw from Iraq but continued to assert our will on the high seas.

As we stared at each other, a thousand thoughts flashed through my mind, none of them good. I just kept watching the guy's eyes.

After a few tense moments, the boat suddenly sped off. I lowered our alert status, and we all breathed a little easier.

But in that situation, you can never be sure the potential hostile isn't just faking you out before coming back, so you never really relax. The tension lingers in the back of your mind. That's what made those watches so stressful.

Halfway through the deployment, the Commanding Officer reassigned me from weapons officer—where my responsibilities included maintaining the readiness of our various mounted weapons and even sidearms—to combat information center officer. This put me in a secret space on the ship, with locked doors that offered extremely limited access. In this room, crew members manned radar, sonar, and other important devices, dominated by two big screens that could be used for video chats with fleet command and other vessels about mission objectives and other sensitive information. I enjoyed this assignment. It was both challenging and fun.

Six-hour shifts in a dark room can be very taxing, however, and the conversations you fall into at three o'clock in the morning can be quite interesting.

I loved the Navy and was proud to serve my country. It was one of the most fulfilling and rewarding experiences of my life. Those challenging days on active duty in the fleet helped me grow into the man I am today.

But a fire raged inside me.

I was torn between two worlds.

During my off-duty hours, my mind often wandered to my first love back home. I was desperately trying to figure out how to chase my dream of playing professional baseball and do right by the Navy.

The clock was ticking on my opportunity to make something out of my baseball talent.

Baseball was part of me, and I couldn't let it die without a fight.

***

Several weeks after graduation, I was staying with my parents at their house in Maryland while awaiting my orders.

Thinking hard about my situation, I didn't want to show up for my first assignment as an athlete just trying to get out of his commission. I didn't want to get that reputation. So, when I got my orders for the Ponce and my reporting date, I called up our executive officer, Frank Gianocaro, the second-ranking officer behind the ship's captain.

"Sir, I just want to introduce myself…"

He interrupted me. "I know who you are."

This surprised me. I didn't know whether this was good or bad, but I kept going.

"Sir, the reason why I'm calling is, I don't want you to think you will have any issues with me..."

After explaining my determination to be a good officer, I arranged to meet with Captain Tim Crone and the XO several days before I was scheduled to report to Norfolk. Both were Naval Academy grads.

Laying it on the line, I explained, "I do want to play baseball, as soon as I possibly can. But I know that by being a dirtbag, it's not gonna help. I want to do my job here and to do it well."

They listened to me, and both said they respected my situation.

"Look," Captain Crone said, "we have no problem with that. As long as you come on and do what's expected of you, we'll help you."

True to their word, my two superiors supported me when I compiled and submitted a multi-page appeal to the Secretary of the Navy.

With the captain's backing, Gianocaro spent hours and hours helping me fill out the voluminous paperwork, asking the Navy to help me find a solution that would allow me to play baseball while still fulfilling my service commitment.

Several other service academy graduates around my age were being granted waivers, including West Point's Cole White, who was drafted in the sixth round by the Kansas City Royals. In 2010, the Army granted White an early release, after serving only two years of his five-year commitment.

My package was carefully written and respectful, and I figured it was only a matter of time before someone in the Navy brass latched onto the obvious publicity benefits of my situation.

The possibility of somehow, someday playing professional baseball occupied my thoughts, especially during those lonely nights at sea.

Often, I manned the late watch alongside a group that included Operations Specialist Second Class Mike Alvarez.

Talking about my dream somehow made it real, and Alvarez indulged me as we discussed the game and wondered what the big leagues would be like if I ever made it.

"Mitch had the skills to do something that so many of us wished we could do but would he ever get the chance. We talked a lot about it, and I watched him struggle with the situation," Alvarez said.

In lighter moments, two guys from the U.S.A. surrounded by nothing but water, he used to give me crap: "Hey, Mitch, you're in the middle of the Gulf right now, and you could be making $500,000 a week playing baseball!"

One of the great things about the American military is that it attracts people from all sorts of backgrounds, united by the desire to serve and to chase a little piece of the American Dream.

Every person on that ship had a dream.

No doubt, some wanted to make admiral.

Others wanted to own their own business.

A few talented musicians fantasized about performing before cheering crowds.

Some wanted to escape a cycle of poverty to buy a house in a nice neighborhood.

Every dream worth having requires tenacity and a commitment to excellence.

Mine was just a little more public, and a little more complicated.

"Mitch was showing us the power of having a dream and chasing it with everything you've got," Alvarez said. "So many of us were pulling for him."

Utilizing a big bag of baseballs supplied by my father and wearing a favorite glove, I began throwing on the flight deck with a Dominican-born cook.

Culinary Specialist Second Class Victor Nunez loved baseball as much as I did.

"At first I didn't know anything about Mitch being drafted," Nunez said. "We were just two guys throwing a ball back and forth. But it didn't take me long to see that he was really good."

Sometimes we stayed out there for hours, just two guys sharing a very American ritual while surrounded by the blue expanse of the gulf.

It was a great distraction.

Eventually, I showed him my draft letter from the Cardinals.

"We spent a lot of time talking about what he wanted to do when he got out of the Navy," Victor said. "I tried to encourage him, keep him thinking positive, and told him to throw it as hard as he could—and he did. Sometimes that little regular glove that I had was really smoking, he threw so hard."

One little slip, though, and the ball was gone.

"We lost a lot of balls," Victor said.

We missed a few that caught the wind and went into the drink, and some others landed errantly on the hard flight deck and bounced violently into the water.

Sometimes a crowd would gather, cheering me on —to see how hard I could throw.

The routine kept my arm somewhat active, but I think the benefit proved to be more psychological than physical.

Remember Steve McQueen's character in *The Great Escape*?

Every time the Germans tossed the American pilot into the cooler, he had his baseball and his glove. The thwack of him methodically bouncing the ball against the wall of his cell was the sound of his defiance. They could put him in solitary confinement, but they couldn't break him.

The baseball player trapped inside me kept telling the Naval officer to stay tenacious and patient.

Half a world away from Busch Stadium, Fenway Park, and Wrigley Field, tossing the ball across that long flight deck kept the game alive in my head.

My spirit was increasingly defiant.

But my body was getting older by the day.

***

Several months before my first deployment, while starting to make connections around Virginia Beach, I met a beautiful young woman through mutual friends at church, and we hit it off and started dating. Let's call her Jane.

When I returned from the Persian Gulf, she stood waiting on the pier in Norfolk for me, alongside my mom, dad, and sisters.

What a great feeling.

My life was starting to shape up nicely.

"She came from a great family," Mom said. "The more time we spent together, the more we liked her."

We had about two months of quality time before my next deployment, and this allowed us to get closer and closer. I fell hard for her and was madly in love.

After returning from my second deployment, we married in 2010 and moved into a high-rise apartment in Virginia Beach.

It was tough when I left on my third deployment several months later, but it was good to know that I had someone waiting for me to get home.

When the Navy rejected my first appeal to play baseball, leaving me with no real answers and no concrete hope for the future, Jane saw my frustration and began encouraging me to find contentment in my life as a Naval officer. She didn't really understand what I was chasing, or why, and wanted me to move on.

But at least some of the pieces of my life were starting to fall into place. We were very happy, and we had started to talk about having children.

The day I left for my third and longest deployment, aboard the U.S.S. Carr, we both cried. We were that close, that invested in each other.

The Carr (FFG-52) was a 4,100-ton Perry class frigate, commissioned in 1985. It was 453 feet long, could accommodate fifteen officers and 190 enlisted crew, and capable of carrying two SH-60 LAMPS III helicopters. Much bigger and faster than the Ponce, it could exceed 29 knots, powered by two massive General Electric turbines.

I developed a great rapport with my commanding officer, Captain Patrick Kulokowski, who recalled me as someone who "stood out among the JOs (junior officers)."

"A lot of guys are perfectly content to go through their JO careers just reacting, doing what they're told, but Mitch was a guy who wanted...to make things better," he said. "You could see him thinking through things, and trying to bring added value to a situation."

The Academy had trained me to lead, and I understood the importance of initiative and critical thinking.

The captain was struck one day not too long after we sailed from Norfolk when we were on the bridge and I confidently said, "Sir, I've got this. I've been trained. I've got it."

He looked me over and gave me the opportunity to prove myself.

"That's when Mitch sort of popped out of the background, and I watched him and knew he was very capable," Kulokowski said. "He was probably the boldest in the water, and as a captain, that sort of confidence and ability is what you want to see."

My confidence came mostly from having watched him, observing how he took control of the ship. By this point in my development, I knew I was one of the best and that I could handle the situation.

It didn't take him long to understand that I wasn't just an athlete trying to mark time on the water.

"I know Mitch was frustrated about the baseball situation, but he wasn't a guy who was wanking about it all the time," he said. "He was a good officer who was just sort of trudging along, doing what he was supposed to do. Baseball was in the background. You wouldn't know about it if you didn't get to know him pretty well."

He wound up helping me file two separate appeals to play baseball.

We started out this sea tour, my last, on what amounted to a goodwill mission to Russia and the Baltic States of Estonia, Latvia, and Lithuania as well as Finland, then sailed into the Arctic Circle.

The so-called Blue Nose initiation for those of us crossing into the Arctic for the first time was memorable. You never forget your first time at the top of the world.

Eventually, after stopping in England and Miami, we worked our way down to the Caribbean and the South Atlantic, where our mission was to assist with intelligence-gathering and interdiction of the illicit drug trade.

Patrolling waters near Columbia, the Carr spent significant time identifying and tracking suspicious vessels.

We were involved in a game of cat-and-mouse with the smugglers, and command often used us to determine which flag a ship was flying and other details that required a close-up view. Often, they switched flags in the middle of a voyage and traveled erratically to confuse authorities.

One day, orders came to chase one ship down, while working with the United States Coast Guard.

The pursuit was frantic, and after pulling up beside the suspicious vessel and working through our rules of engagement, the Coast Guard decided we should board it. The captain of the other ship knew better than to resist.

After searching the ship, the Coast Guard found millions of dollars of cocaine, hidden behind cement-covered walls in the belly of the ship.

Everyone wanted a picture standing in front of that massive haul.

After taking the crew into custody and chaining their ankles to a wire in an isolated area of the Carr, we carefully retrieved the cocaine and loaded it onto our ship. Then we blew up the outlaw ship, which quickly sank to the bottom of the Atlantic.

One prisoner tested positive for tuberculosis and needed to be quarantined, so our crew chained him to an area on deck and then built a covering that resembled an awning, for his protection, as we sailed for Guantanamo Bay, Cuba.

This served as a reminder to us all: Even in the middle of the nasty business of trying to impede the international narcotics trade, we were the good guys, and the Navy would treat even these drug peddlers as humanely as possible.

By this point, Gitmo was notorious among our enemies, and one guy pleaded with us for mercy.

"This is the only way I had to make money for my family," he insisted through an interpreter. "What choice did I have?"

It wasn't hard to feel sympathy for such individuals ensnared by the power of a drug cartel and likely paid peanuts to take all the risks, but they faced many years of incarceration.

Knowing that the crew of the Carr had made a little dent in the drug trade that was wrecking so many American lives was gratifying. But we were ordered to deliver the cocaine to the Colombian government, which left me and many others with a hollow feeling.

What? Are you serious? That doesn't make sense. You know it's going right back to the cartel!

Were we really making a difference, or was this just a Pyrrhic victory in a never-ending war?

6

One Dark Night

ABOUT HALFWAY THROUGH THE deployment, I realized something was wrong.

Jane sounded different.

The ability to make telephone calls home was limited, so while on the ship, we mostly communicated through email.

When I placed the occasional phone call to Virginia, the conversations felt increasingly distant. It sounded like she really didn't want to speak with me, which was strange, because I was thousands of miles away and you would think that your wife would be happy, even excited, to hear your voice. She always sounded like she needed to cut the conversation short.

At the same time, her responses to my frequent emails felt abbreviated and less personal.

Sometimes you just know.

Sensing that the distance weighed on her, I tried to explain that I too felt frustrated—expressing how much I wished I could be home and how much I was looking forward to being with her again.

But this line of talk didn't move the needle.

"What's going on with you?" I finally asked in an email.

"What's wrong?"

"What have I done?"

"Why can't you communicate with me?"

She refused to give me a straight answer.

The not knowing drove me crazy.

In the military, you become intimately familiar with the age-old stories about the man going overseas for months at a time and his lonely woman falling into the arms of another. We joke about this sort of thing. There's even a cadence about a cheating military spouse.

But now I was beginning to think the unthinkable about Jane, which motivated me to engage in some long-distance surveillance.

With online access to our joint cell phone bill, I devoted some of my down time on the ship to carefully sifting through the call log.

One number had been called repeatedly rather late at night, and I didn't recognize it.

After letting the situation stew in my mind for a couple days, I placed a call to the number. No one answered. The voice mail greeting was a man's voice, and I took note of his name.

Later, I sent Jane an email: "Who is this person?"

In a subsequent phone call, I confronted her about this man and told her I could see from our bank statements that she had made a trip to North Carolina without mentioning it, which was not like her.

"I know something is going on!" I said, and asked her to explain.

She insisted that the man in question was a just friend from work, someone she admired, before starting to turn it around on me: "What are you doing going through our phone records? Why don't you trust me?"

The situation continued to deteriorate, and finally, with about three weeks left in our deployment, I went to my CO to request an early leave.

"Once I found out he was having some problems at home, I gave him a chance to go back," Captain Kulokowski said.

We slowly made our way back from the South Atlantic, and I got off the ship in Florida and caught a flight home to Virginia.

Maybe I can salvage the situation.

When I called to tell Jane I was coming home two weeks early—which meant we could celebrate our first anniversary—she didn't seem the least bit excited. Instead, she wanted to know: "Why are you coming home early?"

The scene at the airport was beyond frosty.

After pulling her car up to the terminal, she didn't even get out to greet me. I tossed my bags in the car and got in on the front passenger side, and she gave me sort of a half-hug, while keeping one hand on the steering wheel. It was not the sort of homecoming you would expect from a wife who hadn't seen her husband in months.

I was determined to get to the bottom of the situation, and to see what I could do to fix it, but she started berating me for "snooping" on her. It went downhill from there. She kept evading my questions.

When we got to our condo, she made it perfectly clear that she didn't feel "comfortable" sleeping with me in our bed.

Comfortable.

She didn't feel comfortable sleeping with her husband.

On our first anniversary, I slept on the couch.

***

When I decided to tell my story, I knew I needed to tell it all, and that this would require looking deep inside myself to reveal and examine some incredibly painful truths.

I had bottled emotions and thoughts inside me for years, and telling my story has proven therapeutic for me.

I'm opening up my guts because you need to understand that my story reflects some higher truths: Success isn't always a rocket ride to fame and fortune. Chasing a dream often takes tremendous sacrifice and struggle. Often, it requires you to confront debilitating darkness and paralyzing doubt.

I sincerely hope that my story will inspire others to reach for big dreams—undaunted by long odds.

This is a book for anyone who has ever aspired to do something that seemed impossible. Anyone who has ever been told "no." Anyone who has ever felt lost. Anyone who has ever drifted perilously close to the edge while stumbling around in the dark.

All these descriptions once applied to me.

To fully appreciate the historic achievement of April 25, 2015, you need to understand the lonely and desperate period that preceded it.

To be honest, it hurts me to go back there, back to the man I once was, but you need to hear this part of the story too if you want to understand who I am now and how I got here from there.

Jane never believed in my baseball dream, but in the early days at least, she seemed to understand how important it was to me—and how important it was that she didn't actively undermine and ridicule my pursuit.

Then, this suddenly changed.

When I returned home on leave, her attitude became aggressively mocking. Clearly, she was determined to hit me where it truly hurt.

"It's never going to happen!" she insisted. "You're just wasting your time!"

This was like a dagger twisting deep into my heart.

Imagine the woman you love suggesting you are building your life on one gigantic delusion.

When she started talking this way—using my dream as a weapon against me—I should have known it was over.

After recently receiving my second denial from the Navy, I tried to keep the faith, leaning hard on mental toughness and tenacity.

I was a warrior who thought and acted as a warrior.

But by loving Jane, I had given her the power to reach through all that strength to make me doubt myself, if only in a rare, fleeting moment of weakness, when my whole world shattered into little pieces.

What if she is right?

What if I'm wasting my time?

***

Eventually I became convinced that Jane hadn't been wasting her time.

The morning after our anniversary, she slept late, and I noticed her digital camera. I flipped it open and saw all these pictures with this same guy at several different hiking areas in North Carolina. These were areas I recognized confirmed by basic detective work on the internet.

She refused to admit what I could clearly see, but then after a few minutes of silence finally said, "I don't love you anymore."

My heart just smashed onto the floor.

Could this really be happening?

Coming from a loving Christian home, I wrestled with this sudden turn of events.

Were we really headed for a divorce?

Suddenly, guilt washed over me—I had been away for so much of our marriage.

"What can I do?" I pleaded, and then suggested we go to counseling.

She gave me a nasty look. "I don't need counseling."

But I pushed back. "You pick the counselor, and I'll pay for it! I'll do whatever!"

I tried to insist that we see a Christian counselor, but she picked someone outside the faith system, the same person who had talked her good friend's mother into a divorce.

As I confided in my father on the phone, he could hear the pain in my voice.

"Mitch was absolutely heartbroken," Dad said. "And I felt so powerless. There was nothing I could do to make him feel any better."

We went to counseling once, giving Jane an opportunity to proclaim that she no longer loved me in front of a complete stranger. Talk about devastating. That's a special kind of lonely, when the woman you love treats you that way.

My maternal grandfather used to tell me that men don't cry. I love him to death, but I completely disagree. Real men should be able to acknowledge and show their emotions.

Listening to my wife speak about me with absolutely no affection in front of this counselor, I broke down and started bawling. I had never felt so low in all my life.

***

One night after Jane moved out of our condo, I packed a duffel bag and walked into the night, headed for my truck, away from all those memories. I had been drinking heavily for several days.

Baseball seemed increasingly out of reach, and my marriage barreled toward divorce. Soon I would transition to shore duty for the last eighteen months of my Navy commitment.

My life was quickly spiraling out of control.

I didn't know where I was going, but I just had to get out of there—away from the bed where I had spent all those intimate moments with my wife, away from the couch where I'd slept fitfully on our first anniversary.

Tucked into the bag was my .45 caliber handgun. It was loaded.

For the first time in my life, I grappled with my faith. At my lowest moment, I began to feel that God had abandoned me. That's difficult for a music minister's son to say, but it's true.

Praying on the matter, I struggled to understand: *Why is He putting me through all this pain? What do I really believe?*

Looking back on that moment now, I can clearly see yet another example of God's intervention in my life. He pushed me to my wit's end to prove He was in control. It was like He was telling me: "I'm going to let you wander down this dark path until you figure out that you have to trust Me."

I didn't realize it at that point, but my desperation represented a kind of surrender. Walking to my truck, I felt lost and alone, the pain fighting for control.

What's it going to hurt if I just put this gun between my teeth and pull the trigger? Who would really care?

I'll never know if I would have used it, but I know my irrational thoughts left me very vulnerable to making one fatefully bad decision.

And then God sent me an angel to pull me back from the edge.

My phone rang at the exact right time, just as I opened the door.

It was Mom. She didn't know about the gun, but she knew I was in a bad way.

"I could tell Mitchell was crying when he picked up the phone, and it was just so unlike him, so I said, 'What are you doing?'" Mom recalled.

"I don't know."

She could tell I was outside and then heard the door slam shut on my truck.

"What do you mean you don't know? Are you headed out?"

There was a lengthy pause on my end of the line.

"Yeah, but I don't know where I'm going."

Now she was really getting worried.

"Okay. It's probably not a good idea to get on the highway if you don't know where you're going."

Looking back, Mom said, "We were a long way away, and he sounded despondent. He wasn't thinking right. I knew all I could do was try to convince him to go somewhere where he would be safe."

Deeply concerned but trying not to overreact, Mom eventually convinced me to go see my friend Jerry (not his real name), who happened to be my soon-to-be ex-wife's brother.

This struck me as a good idea, so I texted Jerry, and a few minutes later, I pulled up to his house, doing my best to hide my red-from-crying eyes. My grandfather's voice echoed through my head, and I sure didn't want my buddy to know that I had been sobbing.

We spent half the night talking and drinking, and I felt a little better before passing out on his couch.

And I made it through that awful night.

***

The phone call was a turning point, but it didn't cause me to immediately abandon my self-destructive path. That would take time.

As we moved toward divorce, I was desperately trying to treat the pain with heavy doses of alcohol, random women, and reckless rides on my recently purchased Harley-Davidson motorcycle, burdened with some pretty dark thoughts.

No longer a controlled social drinker who tended to have no more than a few beers with my buddies, I was getting wasted several nights a week on hard liquor. The casual sex enabled the drinking, and the drinking enabled the casual sex.

After a while, I mostly felt numb.

During this separation phase, I went after any girl who showed me the least amount of attention. Desperately craving intimacy—a hunger compounded by months of distance from my wife during deployment—I wasn't at all picky.

It was more than the sex. I also needed the validation of the conquest, some pretty girl to pick me and agree to go back to my condo, because my self-esteem was basically circling the bottom of the toilet.

Meanwhile, Jane was playing silly games, refusing to file for the divorce she clearly wanted. Eventually, I would have to file the paperwork myself. But for months, I kept thinking that just maybe, she would have a change of heart, and we would get back together.

***

Even as I mourned the demise of my marriage, her words still haunted me.

What if she was right? What if I'm wasting my time chasing this ridiculous, impossible dream?

It was hard to keep this thought buried deep, but it persisted, taunting me, wrestling for control.

In those moments of weakness, baseball was just another once-tangible thing that now seemed destined to break my heart.

Especially after the Navy rejected my second petition, I began to feel increasing bitterness toward the Navy bureaucracy.

I was serving my country honorably and complied with all that the Navy had asked of me.

During that period, while struggling with my personal demons and the breakup of my marriage, I was also fighting my own private war against the Navy bureaucracy.

No one at the Pentagon seemed willing to listen to my plea.

"Mitch was so frustrated," Dad said. "I just don't think they understood what great PR they could have gotten out of him playing baseball. He was in his prime, and the Cardinals wanted him. We kept thinking they would find a way to work it out where he could do right by the Navy but get to live out his dream."

Why couldn't we work something out?

Why were others granted waivers and not me?

These thoughts and others rattled around my head on a constant loop.

"It would have been real easy in those days for Mitch to give up," Dad said. "But he kept fighting, kept believing it would all work out eventually."

Of course, Jane wanted me to give up, and I certainly wasn't going to give her the satisfaction of being proven right.

But another, more fundamental reason kept me in the fight.

At this point, I desperately needed baseball more than ever. It was all I had, and I wasn't sure who I would become if I surrendered. It was like the last penny in my pocket and the last song in my heart, so I held tightly to the intoxicating idea of it, held on for dear life.

***

While I tried to pull myself out of the big black hole, Mom sent me a hand-written letter with a printed copy of the Bible's book of James. It certainly stimulated my thinking, especially the emphasis on struggle and perseverance.

I was still wrestling with my faith, still wrestling with who I was, but instead of pushing God away, at my parents' suggestion, I began to see a Christian counselor.

After we talked for a while, he could see I was having a hard time coming to grips with one particular aspect of my marriage. All of my life up to that point, I had excelled at everything that was important to me: High school. Baseball. The Academy. The Navy.

Now I had failed, and didn't know how to handle it.

My counselor taught me to look at the situation in a different way, understanding that I wasn't responsible for Jane's behavior or her sudden realization that she no longer loved me.

I couldn't control her, but I could control the way I reacted to the situation.

This was an important step in moving forward, and he was very good at getting me to open up and think.

One day he gave me some sage advice: "You need to write this stuff down."

Me?

A journal?

What am I, a poet?

That's not who I am.

"I'll just go ride my Harley when I feel the walls closing in," I told him.

But he insisted, pushing me to buy a notebook.

"You need to get it out," he said. "It will help. You'll see."

Reluctantly, I started putting pen to paper, often after a night of heavy drinking, especially if I came home alone.

Late one night, pretty wasted, I sat in my condo with the TV blaring and a half-empty bottle of booze on the coffee table. My despair now compounded my obsession over some girl who was no longer returning my texts.

Apparently, I had been ghosted.

I didn't care about her, but that wasn't the point. She was a warm body, someone to make me feel alive, and I was lonely.

Maybe she never really liked me.

Maybe no girl will ever really like me again.

One doubt leads to others, and suddenly it's raining negative thoughts in your head.

Feeling like a total loser, I picked up my notebook and started reading through the thoughts I had jotted down, often stream-of-consciousness style. One recent passage caught my eye. I read it over and over, and something stirred inside me. *Whoa, that's deep! Who wrote that?*

In that moment, I felt God reaching out to me, as if He was saying, "Sober up for a minute. I'm trying to tell you that you have the courage to face this..."

Suddenly, I got an idea and fumbled for my phone.

Within a few minutes, I sat in an all-night tattoo parlor, just another bleary-eyed Navy guy searching for meaning at the end of a needle.

The artist pulled a drag on his cigarette and said, "What you want?"

I took out a piece of paper and wrote:

IT TAKES COURAGE TO FACE THE MOUNTAIN AND
STRENGTH TO CLIMB. BUT WHEN YOU REACH THE

SUMMIT AND SEE THE VALLEY, YOU'LL REALIZE WHO
YOU'VE BECOME.

He looked it over. "Hey, man, this is pretty good! Has this been your
life's motto?"

"No. I wrote it earlier tonight."

He smiled.

Consciously or not, Psalms 23 had influenced my thinking, but I
don't think the tattoo artist made the connection.

He started the two-and-a-half-hour process of tattooing my new
mission statement across my ribs.

Embracing those words as I started to sober up, I began to develop
a newfound clarity about my situation. I could either wallow around
in despair or acknowledge the incredible challenge I was facing and
resolve to conquer it, step by harrowing step. In that moment, I chose to
be defiant. In that moment, I chose to fight against my circumstances.

Of course, I didn't have any idea how high that mountain really was.

7

Hope on the Horizon

SEVERAL WEEKS AFTER MY marriage crumbled, I started talking to my commanding officer about attacking my baseball problem from a different direction.

From the start, Captain Kulokowski had been very supportive of my obsession.

He understood that if I didn't pull out all the stops, if I didn't pursue every avenue, I would probably second-guess myself forever.

"Something you've dreamed about your whole life...I totally understood what was driving Mitch and was happy to try to help him, as long as we could do it the right way," said Kulokowski, who endorsed the package I submitted to the Navy in 2011.

"Did I think it was possible? After being away from the game that long? Honestly, I thought it was a pipe dream."

Still, the captain was glad he had me sign a baseball one day on our frigate. It became a treasured keepsake to him.

Working the problem, I sought his advice: What if I applied for a temporary duty transfer to a recruiting office in Florida?

This way maybe I could figure out how to participate in spring training with the Cardinals in 2012, while my latest request for dismissal worked its way through the Navy bureaucracy.

"I'm gonna wave you off on that, Mitch," Kulokowski said.

He could see the disappointment written all over my face.

Discussing this plan many years later, he said, "The TDY thing would have been special treatment that nobody else was getting. I couldn't just let him go play baseball. That wouldn't have ended well for him or for me."

But the captain had his own idea.

"How much leave you got?"

The wheels started turning.

Every Naval officer received thirty days' leave each year, and the Navy didn't care how we used it. Why would playing baseball be any different than sitting on some beach with music playing and an ice-cold drink?

After clearing the strategy with the captain's direct superior, who supported the idea, and talking to the Cardinals, who invited me to spring training, I arranged to save up my leave for the year.

No one would cut any corners for me, and I didn't want to avoid any of my duties or hide my vacation plan.

Still trying to avoid feelings of negativity, still carrying the heavy baggage of my soon-to-be-ex-wife's insistence that my dream was nothing but a big delusion, I was determined to find a way forward and to prove all the doubters wrong—especially her.

Finally getting back onto a baseball field for that month at the Cardinals' spring training facility in Jupiter, Florida, was a blast. It felt so good to put on a uniform and feel the dirt under my feet again, to stand on the mound, plant my feet and unload a fastball into the distance. But it didn't take me long to understand the impact of all that inactivity on my once-powerful arm.

In Annapolis, the radar guns had consistently clocked me in the mid-90s.

Now they told a sad story.

Eighty-four.

That was my max number now.

Eighty-four.

The number felt like a lead weight dangling from my neck.

No way was eighty-four going to get me anywhere near the big leagues.

You could tell the other up-and-coming pitchers, the young guys with the electric arms, guys propelled by their own animated fantasies of Major League glory, heard my number and privately wondered, *What is that guy doing here? Who is he kidding?*

The Cardinals and Major League Baseball happily capitalized on the good publicity of an active-duty Naval officer chasing his elusive baseball dream, and several reporters picked up on the story, flooding me with interviews that always struck a patriotic chord. But under the circumstances, I started to feel like a gimmick, like I was being patronized.

They did everything but pat me on the head.

But at least I could do what I loved and start to put all the anguish of 2011 behind me.

News of my activity reached the Pentagon, and someone from fleet forces called Kulokowski.

"It was a pretty high-level call: 'What do you mean Mitch Harris is playing baseball at spring training?'" the captain recalled. "I said, 'Well, he's on leave.'"

The officer on the other end of the line paused and finally said, "Okay. I guess that's alright."

About two weeks later, my cell phone rang in Florida.

The Pentagon had denied my request. Again. No explanation. Just another denial.

To make matters worse, on the very same day, Eric Kettani, a former star fullback for the Navy football team, had been approved to play for the New England Patriots. Kettani was a friend, and I was happy for him, but why him and not me?

Devastated, I placed a call to someone at the Pentagon acquainted with my situation, looking for an explanation for why I was being treated differently.

But no one could tell me why.

***

Not long after I returned to Norfolk and my shore duty on the U.S.S. Carr, trying not to feel deflated, I received a call from an old friend. Sean and I had grown up together in Georgia, playing on the same baseball teams, our families attending the same church. We caught up a bit, and he told me that he was thinking about pursuing a career in the military. He asked me to share my experiences and offer some advice.

The conversation about the military continued over the next couple of weeks, which led inevitably to connections on Facebook, where I enjoyed catching up on the photos of people I had once known pretty well.

He appreciated my advice, and I was happy to help him understand the great things about the military as well as the various adjustments that he would face.

During one of our conversations, Sean veered off topic.

"Mitch, I know this is going to sound weird but..."

He asked if I remembered his little sister, Mandi.

"Sure."

The girl I remembered from Lawrenceville was a seven-year-old tomboy, about four years younger than me, when we were playing paintball or some other sport in one of our backyards.

Sean started talking about all the losers she had dated and then suggested that we might hit it off.

By this point, my divorce was in progress but would not be finalized for several months yet. My time of debauchery at the Norfolk bars was beginning to wind down, starting to lose its power to make me feel better. I wasn't drinking as much and wasn't spending my nights wallowing in self-pity.

Slowly, I was pushing Jane out of my system, even though she would contact me from time to time to play silly little games, trying to get me back, which made it even tougher for me to move on.

Maybe I was ready for a nice girl with potential.

Logging onto Facebook, I caught a glimpse of his little sister and felt immediately impressed and interested. She looked really good, all grown up.

Meanwhile, Sean was working on his sister.

"My brother texted me at seven o'clock in the morning, when I was on the way out the door, headed to work," Mandi recalled years later. "He said, 'I just had this great insight. I think you and Mitch Harris should talk.'"

Mandi and I connected on Facebook, which led to a long phone call to her in Atlanta. Pretty soon, we were talking on the phone just about every night, sometimes for two or three hours. We didn't actually start hanging out in person until I had finalized my divorce.

"Early on, I learned that his wife had hurt him pretty badly and was still trying to manipulate him," Mandi said. "He would call me and tell me about her coming up to him when he was in his truck, and she would start crying. At one point I just told him, 'You need to understand that she may be crying to you, trying to get sympathy or whatever, but she's going to sleep in the bed with that other guy.' Mitch has such a good heart, he was still torn, trying to do the right thing."

It had been nearly a year since Jane ripped my world into little pieces on the night of our anniversary, and I had built this massive wall to protect myself from another broken heart.

Letting go was a multi-stage process, and so was learning to trust another human being, and Mandi helped me negotiate these difficult and painful transitions.

For our first date, I took her to a Luke Bryan concert.

We had our first kiss over the banana pudding she made just for me.

***

Two or three months into my relationship with Mandi, I meticulously prepared another thick packet asking the Navy to allow me to play baseball.

She didn't tell me I was wasting my time.

In my letter, I respectfully pointed out that I had served three overseas deployments and tried to do all the right things.

But I made it clear that, if they didn't grant me a waiver this time, my dream might slip away for good.

My body was aging rapidly, and while I had many years to serve proudly as a Naval officer, baseball was a young man's game.

Then one phone call changed my life.

As I hung out with my friend Carmine Vozza at our condo in Virginia Beach, my cell rang.

It was December 2012, and an official who had reviewed my paper-work wanted to let me know that the Navy was allowing me to leave active duty at the end of January, about four months early. As part of the agreement, I would serve three years in the Navy Reserves, instead of the customary two, which had been one of my suggestions in my previous appeals with the Pentagon brass.

Carmine heard my side of the conversation, and as soon as I hung up the phone, we both literally jumped for joy.

Could this really be happening?

After confirming an invitation to spring training with the Cardinals, in a phone conversation with Director of Baseball Administration John Vuch, I started making plans to head to Florida a little early to whip myself into shape.

The family of Mark McCoy, my Academy teammate, lived in Boca Raton, and generously allowed me to crash at their place for several weeks before the minor league camp started. It took forty minutes to drive to the Cardinals complex in Jupiter, so every morning, I got up early and made that drive, worked out for the majority of the day, and then drove back to Boca.

McCoy was a good friend, and he was pulling for me.

Years later, I would learn that he doubted me, like many others.

Mark was one of my biggest fans. But still, he wondered if I was being delusional.

"There was no way he was going to make it," McCoy said, looking back on those days. "No way. Plain and simple: He was a PR story for the Cardinals."

Watching video of me throwing, he thought, *Mitch's arm doesn't work anymore.*

Of course he was right.

My arm was not the same.

But the question was: Could I somehow bring it back to life?

McCoy was torn between encouraging me to relentlessly chase my dream and forcing me to face a harsh reality.

At the time, I was sleeping in Mark's childhood bedroom, living on my savings and getting rocked every day by guys who wondered what the hell I was doing out there.

"Part of me was thinking, *Should we do some sort of intervention?*" McCoy recalled. "*Do we need to find this guy a job? How do we make sure Mitch lands on his feet?*"

You have to understand that, at this point, I had never experienced an off-season in professional baseball and had never learned how to prepare for spring training. This was a big weakness in my game, all because I had been living on a ship for nearly five years. Yes, I was pushing hard on the activity scale, doing whatever I could to work myself into better shape but not accomplishing much, which soon became painfully obvious.

My ceiling was still 84 miles per hour.

In various other ways, I looked like a party crasher, but that number alone would disqualify me. If I couldn't find my old velocity, my dream would slip away for good.

Pitching coach Jason Simontacchi still remembers watching me throw during the first day of camp, not yet acquainted with my story, not yet invested in my dream.

"He was not throwing hard at all," Simontacchi said, and he couldn't help but wonder why.

Walking up to talk with me, he quickly learned that I had been away from baseball for nearly five years and that I was understandably concerned about my arm.

Remarking on the situation all these years later, he said, "In our business, you learn not to judge people too quickly. Some things take time. But you also learn not to fall in love with anybody. It can fog your judgment."

He could see I was frustrated and urged me to be patient, reminding me that arm strength can be regained under the right circumstances.

"Dude, they invited you here for a reason," he said.

Especially given the demoralizing experience of the previous spring, I had to wonder: Was their reason the same as mine?

I understood the incredibly long odds, but my dream had a heartbeat. It wasn't dead yet.

8

Climbing the Mountain

TO GET ANYWHERE IN life, you need to embrace the power of calculated risk.

Sometimes, this means overcoming sweaty palms and the fear of rejection to ask the pretty girl to dance.

Most guys can relate to such a scenario.

No risk, no reward.

Sometimes this means sinking your life savings into starting your own business.

It takes a special kind of personality to jump off a financial cliff, betting you can fly.

In my case, I threw away a steady career in the Navy—with significant opportunity for advancement—to chase the *possibility* of someday playing in the Major Leagues.

This is very important to understand.

I was trading the sure thing of the Navy for the *chance* of making it to The Show—while shouldering a roughly 80 percent pay cut.

Even if I decided to get out of the Navy, I could still leverage my Academy education. Several of my classmates did so by entering business school, and others transitioned into high-paying careers in corporate America.

Chasing my baseball dream presented a huge risk.

The Cardinals paid me $10,000 to sign my contract, which barely allowed me to pay off my truck and put a few bucks in the bank.

But it was never about the money.

The only guarantee was a shot to prove that I could still play.

This wasn't something I wanted to do. It was something I *had* to do. A primal force drove me forward—a need bubbling up from deep in my soul.

If I didn't do this, if I didn't take this chance, how would I ever know? How would I live the rest of my life, not knowing what might have happened? How would I deal with the regret reverberating across my life?

Of course, I also represented the Navy and the Academy, which added another level of pressure and motivation. I didn't want to let any of those people down.

To chase my elusive dream, I would have to negotiate my way through a complex maze of competition in the St. Louis Cardinals' minor league system, while hoping that my aging arm would somehow regain its previous vitality.

The mountain before me filled up the sky.

But after five years away from the game, I had something to prove—to baseball and to myself.

***

On the first day of minor league spring training in 2013, I felt so incredibly self-conscious.

The Cardinals' complex in Jupiter consists of four fields, with a bullpen of three or four mounds in between two fields.

They put me on a mound throwing to a catcher, and my arm felt so weak. Standing on the rubber, winding up and releasing into the warm, humid Florida air, I threw nothing but junk.

One of the pitching coaches stood behind the catcher with a radar gun. After each pitch, he would call out my number.

"Eighty-two!"

"Seventy-nine!"

"Eighty-one!"

Junk.

After a few minutes, Brent Strom, the minor league pitching coordinator, walked up to me.

"You're so tight! We gotta loosen you up."

"Here's what I want you to do..."

Closely following his instructions, I threw a fastball to the catcher. Then I picked up another ball and chucked it as far as I could—into centerfield on the adjoining diamond. Then I repeated the sequence: Another fastball to the catcher. Another long ball into the field.

I felt like a fool.

The hitters were taking batting practice, and as my balls started soaring overhead like off-course missiles, you could hear their confusion and thinly-veiled mockery.

"Head's up!"

"What in the world is he doing?"

"Here comes another one!"

"Who is this guy?"

The point of this unorthodox exercise was to stretch my arm, by throwing it as far as I could.

Looking back on those days, Strom said, "The body will always accommodate the goal that's required, and in Mitch's case, his time on ship had transformed his body...The general rigor of staying in shape for his obligations in the military...really doesn't translate [to throwin a] baseball. His body had reverted back...We had to overcome five years of a body basically shutting down."

It didn't take Strom and the other coaches long to determine that they needed to pursue a radical approach with me.

Learning from lessons they had learned from engineer Paul Nyman, who revolutionized pitching instruction in the 1990s, the organization's coaches initially concentrated on teaching my body to throw again, without worrying about placement or even velocity.

Some days Strom told me, "I want you to just throw it as hard as you can throw. I don't care if you miss the target by eight feet."

Sometimes I did just that.

This focus on power at the expense of precision required a mental adjustment on my part, but I totally bought in and tried to do everything they asked me to do.

It was all pretty disorienting, but at least I was playing baseball again.

"The only way to learn how to throw hard is to throw hard," said Strom, who would play a key role in the Houston Astros' 2017 World Series championship as pitching coach. "What we had to do was unlock Mitch's body, so what was inside could get out. I knew it was in there. We just had to bring it out."

Jason Simontacchi, who pitched for the Cardinals and the Washington Nationals before moving into coaching, remembered me as "a big strapping dude who clearly had more power under the hood."

But my power needed to be rebuilt and harnessed.

If we didn't succeed, there was no way I would get anywhere near Busch Stadium.

As Dr. George Paletta, the Cardinals' team doctor, noted, "The ligament is a living piece of tissue that responds to stresses and strengthens with stresses. It's just like somebody who lifts weights...For five years it wasn't seeing that kind of stress [so] Mitch had to strengthen the ligament before he could know..."

Focused on "utilizing momentum," Strom led the way as we explored techniques used by javelin throwers and shot-putters, devising various unusual drills. We tried so many things.

"Rotation becomes a huge factor," Strom said. "Being able to rotate quickly and create power through rotational forces."

Other players looked on in amazement, wondering what in the world this guy who couldn't throw more than 84 mph was doing in professional baseball.

Strom convinced the Cardinals to send me to a hot yoga class, which was eye-opening in more ways than one. It certainly helped limber up my body, and the scenery was mighty nice.

It had taken five years for my body to fall out of baseball shape, and the coaches kept reminding me that the process of retraining it could take time.

But all I could hear was the alarm clock pounding in my head.

"You could tell Mitch was really stressed and frustrated but by this point. He had pushed so hard for so long, it was just sort of natural for him to keep pushing," Dad said. "There was such an inner strength to him. He kept believing, when it would have been real easy to give up and accept defeat."

Quitting was the easy way out, and I just couldn't quit.

My arm was still pretty weak, but my will was strong.

When all the prospects lined up to run daily sprints, the coaches sometimes wagered on us, and unbeknownst to me, Strom often whispered to the others, "I'll put $20 on the Academy guy."

He was impressed not only by my athleticism but also by my business-like attitude and my drive to succeed.

"Mitch was surrounded by all these much younger guys, some of them really fast, and he would kick their ass in the drills," Strom said. "He was a max effort guy. He was clearly giving it everything he had because he was trying to make a mark."

The mark I was trying to make was covered by various media outlets, garnering significant positive publicity for baseball and the Navy.

But the more I struggled, the more I wondered, *Are the Cardinals just humoring me because it's a good story?*

***

At the end of spring training, while virtually every other player was assigned to a team, they held me back for extended instruction in Jupiter, alongside a bunch of guys right out of high school. It was pretty embarrassing. I stood out like a sore thumb, and everyone wanted to know, *What are you doing here, grandpa?*

After a couple of weeks, I was assigned to the State College (Pennsylvania) Spikes of the Class A New York-Penn League, where the short season ran from June to September. At age twenty-seven, I was older than all of my teammates. Third baseman Carson Kelly, drafted in the second round the previous June and bound for a measure of success with the Cardinals and three other Major League teams, was eighteen. Our manager, future St. Louis skipper Oliver Marmol, was twenty-six.

"I can't even put into words how anxious I am," I told a reporter before the season.

At times, I felt old. But you know what? I felt happy because I was chasing my dream. That mountain was halfway to the clouds, but at least I could *see* it. I knew it was there. It felt almost comforting to face a difficult reality after all those years of trying to keep the fantasy alive in my head.

I had traded the rather comfortable life of a Navy lieutenant—earning close to $80,000 per year plus perks—to bring home about $800 per month while playing before crowds that sometimes measured in the hundreds, traveling around on buses, and living in third-rate motels with a bunch of guys fresh out of high school and college. Many of my teammates still weren't old enough to legally buy a drink.

Living several miles from the Penn State campus—in the guest room of my sponsor family's house—I made the most of living near a college campus. My divorce was final, and finally playing pro ball, I was determined to celebrate and enjoy myself. There were some very pretty women in State College, many who were attracted to the glimmer of a pro ball player on the make.

But I was also very serious about learning to pitch again.

Just pitch. Put all the other stuff out of your head. Just pitch, and see if you belong.

The Cardinals easily could have jettisoned me after spring training. Clearly a lot of people in and around the organization who had seen me throw in college saw the pitcher I was now and believed I could never approach my old self.

It would have been so easy for me to give up on myself coming out of spring training, and frankly, it would have been so easy for the Cardinals to conclude that I didn't have it anymore. But Strom, for one, was fully invested in my dream. "I will tell you, prayer came into play for me," he said. "I knew how badly Mitch wanted it, and I was praying that it would work out."

I recognized State College as a precious lifeline, but none of us had any illusions. No one had to remind me that we were racing the clock.

Working out of the bullpen, I started throwing strikes and getting guys out.

***

Mandi had entered my life when I was just starting to move on from Jane, and by the time I left the Navy, we had been casually dating for about six months.

"I knew he had been drafted, but when he got his release from the Navy, I didn't really know what was coming in terms of baseball," she recalled. "I didn't really understand what I had signed up for."

She genuinely felt happy for me as I started to slog through the minors, chasing my elusive goal.

"I was all for the dream and believed in him, but the dream wasn't State College," Mandi said. "The dream was the Major Leagues. And it took a certain amount of faith to believe that all of his hard work was going to eventually lead to that dream."

Mandi was focused on her career in inside sales, but she took time to visit me at spring training. Not long after I moved to State College, she spent more than $600 on a plane ticket to come see me. We had a great time.

"Mitch was a lot more sophisticated than the other guys I had dated," Mandi said. "He was such a gentleman and treated me so well, and he started teaching me about wine and stuff like that."

She was all in, but to be honest, I wasn't.

I relished my newfound freedom and still wanted to partake in the spoils of being a single man in professional baseball. I wanted to see her but wasn't ready for a commitment.

Only later would I understand that an unfortunate incident during one of our first dates, when I still lived in Virginia Beach, had disturbed Mandi. For some reason, I had chosen to take her to a bar where this girl who liked me started flirting with me in front of her. I never dated the girl, but apparently, she was into me and got her feelings hurt when I walked in with Mandi. The girl ran off and started crying, and Mandi pulled me outside and started blessing me out.

"If you're going to play games, I'm outta here on the next plane!"

A year later, this memory remained fresh in her mind.

Several weeks after the first visit to State College, she paid me a surprise visit, and it didn't go so well.

"I could tell things were just a bit off," she said later.

After returning home to Atlanta, she confronted me with the situation, and I told her I wanted to take a break. She didn't take the news well.

Mandi had gone through a few bad relationships and was mature enough to know that she needed to call my bluff. "I basically told him: 'If you need a break, then we're done. We don't do breaks.'"

She finally hit me with an ultimatum: "If this continues, I'm gone for good. I want you, but I sure don't need you."

On the phone, I tried to strike a cool tone, but my inner monologue was straight from the cocky dude's handbook.

Who is this girl?

Usually they are crying at this point.

I'm not going to chase her!

When we hung up, we both thought we were done.

But it didn't take me long to realize that I had made a horrible mistake. Thinking back on the conversation, letting it roll over and over in my mind, her hard-lined, principled stand began to impress me.

Who does this girl think she is?

I respect the hell out of that!

And I started to miss her. Terribly.

To be honest, I was scared. As much as I wanted to maintain my precious freedom, mainly my fear of commitment had caused me to push Mandi away. I still had my walls up and wasn't ready to trust anyone yet.

She had met my parents at Thanksgiving, and while Mom and Dad had welcomed her, she could feel a certain distance. It was only natural for them to be skeptical of anyone I brought home for the first time. Jane wasn't just a scar on my heart. She had deeply affected my parents, who were forced to watch me suffer.

"Mandi wanted to know why he wouldn't commit," Mom recalled. "Well, it's pretty simple. I told her, 'He had somebody who's stepped on his heart and broken it into little pieces. He's scared to death. Give him time.'"

Two or three days after our contentious phone call, I called her while on a road trip in New York state. She didn't pick up. The voicemail I left was embarrassing. Basically, I told her I knew I had made a huge mistake and that I wanted her back.

I called twice a day for at least a week. It kept going to voicemail.

"All this time, I was talking to my sister, asking her what to do," Mandi said. "She was saying, 'No! No! Don't give in!'"

But she eventually called me back, and we talked.

We shared a deep connection, and we both knew it.

"If you can prove me wrong, I'll give you another shot," she finally said.

Persistence is a life force, and in love as well as baseball, this quality was leading me home.

***

The turning point with the Spikes happened around midseason. We were playing a game in Batavia, New York, against the Muckdogs. I came out of the bullpen and had a good couple of innings. Nothing special. But after the game, I walked into the clubhouse and noticed the pitching chart tacked up to my locker, which struck me as odd.

The starters who weren't pitching that day routinely sat in the stands and methodically charted our pitches, and those guys normally took the sheet straight to the coaching staff.

Why is the chart on my locker?

For some reason they wanted me to see the chart before it went to the coaches, so I picked it up and started looking at the numbers.

"Oh, wow," I said aloud. "I hit 90 again!"

Several of the guys looked over my shoulder, waiting to see my reaction. They all smiled. "Yeah, you did!"

Everyone on the team knew how hard I had worked.

They knew about many of the highs and many of the lows.

They knew about those lonely moments on the ship, when I desperately tried to keep the dream alive in my head.

They knew about my private war against the Navy bureaucracy.

They understood the humiliation of spring training.

They understood my battle to get my body to do what I wanted it to do.

We talked about a lot of this stuff over beers in little dive bars and in darkened buses headed to and from far-flung little towns—Williamsport, Lowell, Jamestown.

Some of the guys wondered aloud why I would trade a serious military career with a future to live like an aging frat boy, not knowing if tomorrow would ever come.

But when I started talking about the game, and the dream, they understood. They could see the fire in my eyes. They could see what the game meant to me, why I chased it so tirelessly.

Everyone was pulling for me, because everyone loved the game just like me. Watching me fight so hard for it made an impression on every guy who had grown up dreaming of someday walking out into a cheering Major League stadium.

We all faced a difficult and uncertain journey. Some of us would make it, and some of us wouldn't. Some of the best players on the Spikes would never know what it was like to walk into a Major League clubhouse and see their name stitched onto a brand-new jersey, dangling in front of your very own locker. Some of the best among us would never feel those goosebumps, the shiver of excitement that ran up your spine, and we understood that athletic talent was just one part of a complex equation. We all rooted for each other to somehow experience the shining moment that we could hold onto for the rest of our lives.

But at the same time, we were all competitive guys. There were only a few precious tickets to the big leagues, and we all wanted one of those tickets. We lived in a world that required a certain amount of selfishness. You had to be willing to put yourself first—a little counterintuitive for a guy steeped in Navy values. I would have done anything to get to the big leagues.

Looking at the chart, as my new friends surrounded me, I was stunned. It was a tremendous milestone, a little jolt of mathematical evidence that maybe, just maybe...

Ninety was a sweet number.

In the weeks ahead, my progress continued. My control kept getting better and better. By the end of the season, my fastball consistently hit the low-90s.

Appearing in twenty games and finishing with a bullpen-best 0.81 ERA and 29 strike-outs in 33 1/3 innings pitched gave me a jolt of confidence. Giving up only three earned runs all year was quite an accomplishment. The team honored me at the season-ending banquet with the Spikes' leadership award.

"I couldn't have written it any better," I told a local sportswriter. "I told myself I wanted to get through this season. Not just survive, but do as well as I could. I didn't know I'd do this well."

It was a real blow when I wasn't promoted at the end of the year. This was a message, and not a good one.

The train was definitely moving in the right direction, but St. Louis was still a million miles away.

The day after our season ended, with a loss in the league championship series, I was packing my truck in the stadium parking lot when the Cardinals' minor league field coordinator, Mark DeJohn, stopped by to see me. He rolled down his car window and waved me over.

"Look," he said, "I know you're disappointed that we didn't move you up..."

Then he started explaining the organization's rationale for keeping me in rookie league ball, also known as Low A. They wanted to see how my body reacted to a full season of baseball in one place. Now they could better evaluate me.

"You're twenty-seven. You need to think about being in Double A next year..."

Really? Double A?

This was two steps up from rookie league ball. How in the world could I make such a leap in one year?

Trust me, I replayed this conversation in my head countless times over the ensuing months. The Cardinals were telling me they expected me to make a serious move up the food chain. I knew enough not to ask what might happen if I didn't.

***

In the months after the fateful phone call, my protective walls came tumbling down, and Mandi and I grew incredibly close.

After spending Thanksgiving 2013 with my parents, we went to the mall to go Christmas shopping.

Walking through the front door, I turned to her. "Do you want to go look at rings?"

She was floored.

We had talked about marriage but not in any depth, and when I hit her with this life-altering question, she smiled and squeezed my hand. Soon, we stood inside a jewelry store on the other side of the mall, peering through display cases.

But something was wrong. I could sense it.

While eating dinner at the bar at P.F. Chang's, I leaned in close. "Look, I'm not going to lie. You aren't as excited as I thought you would be."

She started telling me that she didn't think we were ready for this step because she didn't believe my parents were ready to accept her as their daughter-in-law.

My heart sank.

Maybe she was right.

That night, we went back to my parents' house, and the four of us wound up in a candid and emotional discussion that lasted for several hours.

Mandi confronted my parents about their attitude toward her, and they both acknowledged how difficult it was for them to get over the situation with Jane and trust another woman in my life.

Up to this point, I hadn't fully understood the impact my pain had exerted on Cy and Cindy. They were still trying to protect me. Some of it was unconscious and none of it was personal toward Mandi, but they were still holding back.

Family was super important to both Mandi and myself, as was our shared Christian faith, and Mandi instinctively knew that we could not hope to build the sort of life that we wanted together unless everyone was on the same page.

"What can I do to earn your trust?" Mandi pleaded.

Desperately trying to make a connection, Mandi opened up about some issues in her own family life and how they had staggered her.

She told my parents how much she loved me.

Mom and Mandi wound up in tears, hugging each other, and slowly, we all started to grow closer.

***

The organization wanted me to rest after the season in State College. When I showed up for minor league spring training in 2014, I could feel myself regressing. It wasn't a good spring.

Once again, I wound up in extended spring, without a minor league assignment, which was pretty demoralizing.

Maybe this isn't going to happen.

Am I wasting my time?

Has the clock run out on my dream?

In a meeting with Gary LaRocque, the Director of Player Development, and Strom, I politely but firmly laid it on the line.

"Look," I said, "if there ever comes a time when I'm just a 'story' for the Cardinals, I want you to release me. If I'm not here for the possibility of making the team and making an impact on the field, I don't want to waste your time, and I don't want you to waste mine.'"

Sometimes walking away is the right call, and at that moment, I was prepared to head out the door and move on from my dream.

Would quitting have killed me? Absolutely. But I couldn't keep banging my head against a brick wall if there was no hope.

After these two decision makers listened to my sincere request, which gave the Cardinals an easy out, Strom broke through the tense silence. "No, Mitch. We believe you have a chance. But you're not ready yet."

Encouraged, I went off to continue work in the instructional league and eventually was assigned to the Class A Palm Beach Cardinals. This high A league was a step up from State College, and I started pitching well.

After an 18-inning road game in Tampa, they moved me up to Double A. This was shocking news, in a good way. After the game somebody handed me a plane ticket, and I caught a late-night flight to Springfield,

Missouri, where I joined the pitching staff for the Springfield Cardinals of the Texas League.

Double A was a whole new ball game.

The Springfield Cardinals played in a beautiful 11,000-seat stadium, and the community showed tremendous support for the team, often filling the place to capacity. The clubhouse had a completely different feel. We had somebody who helped with our bags, and we had a nice buffet from a local restaurant.

Only later would I learn that the Cardinals had sent me to Double A so quickly as a make-or-break proposition. If I didn't immediately adjust to the level of competition and excel, they were prepared to cut me.

The competition was intense. You could feel all those talents humming around you, all those guys just starting to hit their athletic potential, many of them fully capable of getting the call.

We were just two steps from The Show, so for the first time since the Navy accepted my request for early release, the dream started to feel more tangible, especially as my control and velocity began to gather momentum.

A whole new set of teammates became acquainted with my personal quest, and a new group of journalists interviewed me about my unusual journey.

"Obviously, I'm pumped," I told a Springfield reporter. "But...I want to make sure this is another steppingstone. If the end goal isn't to get to the big leagues, I'd be doing it for the wrong reason."

One day after a bullpen session prior to a game in Springfield, our pitching coach, Randy Niemann, former big-league reliever, came over to me. He had seen something. "What was that?" he said. "Did you just figure something out?"

My heart raced because I could feel everything clicking, for the first time. "I don't know. That felt great."

"Well, that was a big-league bullpen! You came in with purpose, you hit every spot..."

Looking back, this electric moment represented an important milepost. It was the end of something and the beginning of something else.

Speaking to a reporter later in 2014, Niemann said, "From where he was in 2013 to now is pretty remarkable."

Media and others close to the game were starting to pay attention—and no longer did I feel like I was involved in a PR stunt.

Still, I would always be the Navy guy, and that was just fine with me.

I didn't want anybody to cut me any slack, but was always happy to talk about the pride I had felt in serving our country.

"There's no doubt the younger guys look up to him," Niemann said. "I make a point of making sure our younger players know where Mitch has been and what he's done."

On the field, my confidence surged as my fastball began to clock consistently around 94–95 mph and I perfected my once-lost cutter.

Toward the end of the season, after pitching 57 1/3 innings with forty-five strikeouts and a 3.92 ERA, the Cardinals promoted me to the Triple A Memphis Redbirds. Suddenly, I was surrounded by names who had appeared on big league rosters.

What a difference a single year can make.

Think about it: In twelve months, I had progressed through three levels—from rookie ball to Triple A.

This is almost unheard of.

Like many others inside the organization, St. Louis manager Mike Matheny began to follow my progress.

"From where he started, as a guy who was pitching in the 80s, it would have been difficult to be very optimistic about his trajectory," Matheny recalled years later. "But then his progression was pretty dramatic. When you get to Triple A, you're knocking on the door, and by the end of [the 2014] season, Mitch was knocking on the door."

***

Determined to keep pushing me, the Cardinals shipped me off to the fall instructional league in Arizona, where I made great strides pitching for the Peoria Javelinas under the guidance of coach Jason Simontacchi.

"Mitch came to us with good stuff, but I could see he was still pushing too hard," Simontacchi said. "It was hindering him a little...We brought him out [to Arizona], so he could see better hitting, but I also spent a lot of time talking to him in the bullpen about the mental side...encouraging him to relax a little out there, not press so hard."

Mandi flew out to visit me when I had a couple days off. I rented a Camaro convertible for us to take a road trip from the Scottsdale area to picturesque Sedona.

We were big on sunsets, and she didn't suspect a thing when we pulled up for dinner at this nice restaurant overlooking the red rocks a short time before sunset.

At the appropriate time, I went down on one knee and pulled out the ring.

Tears streamed down her cheeks as I told her I wanted to spend the rest of my life with her.

The look of sheer joy on her face is something I will never forget.

As you can see by now, our love story is deeply intertwined in my baseball story.

It took more than a reinvigorated arm to make my dream come true. It also took a good woman who was willing and able to heal my broken heart.

Mandi believed in my dream when I needed a partner to believe. She became the antidote to the woman who had poisoned me with all those doubts.

As we headed toward 2015, with my baseball dream finally within reach and the love of my life wearing my ring, I felt like a whole man, perhaps for the first time in my life.

***

Being invited to my first Major League spring training was a great feeling and a good sign.

Maybe the front office expected to ship me back to Triple A Memphis to start the season, but in my mind I was there to make the big league club.

When I showed up in Jupiter in February 2015, the radar guns no longer taunted me, and the pitching coaches no longer labored to squeeze more velocity out of my right arm.

Thanks to two years of painstaking work, incredible faith, and patience from many members of the St. Louis Cardinals organization, my arm was now a weapon I could fully leverage, capable of consistently chucking 95-mph fastballs across the nearest strike zone.

By this time, it was starting to dawn on me how lucky I was to be a part of the Cardinals organization.

St. Louis is one of the best baseball cities in America, with a large base of knowledgeable and loyal fans who have consistently supported the Cardinals for more than a century.

Think about all the amazing teams and great players who have worn the red and white uniform.

Everyone knows that the New York Yankees have won more World Series championships (twenty-seven) than any other franchise, but how many casual fans realize that the Cardinals rank second on this all-time list, with eleven World Series titles plus nineteen National League pennants?

How vividly I remember watching Ozzie Smith scoop up one hard-hit ground ball after another and fire it toward first. He was like a machine and an artist all at once. No shortstop of my youth was more respected or feared, even when he stole a base hit from one of my beloved Braves.

So many of baseball's all-time greatest played for the Cardinals, including Enos "Country" Slaughter, Rogers Hornsby, Lou Brock, Dizzy Dean, Ted Simmons, John Smoltz, Albert Pujols, Larry Walker, and Stan Musial.

Growing up wanting to pitch, and later having access to old video on my laptop and smartphone, I especially admired the legendary Bob Gibson, one of the most intimidating pitchers who ever stepped on a mound.

One day during spring training in 2015, I was sitting by myself in the dugout. It was my rest day, so no pitching for me. But I liked being around the action.

Since my days as a two-way player in college, I enjoyed hanging out in the dugout to watch the other guys on the field and seeing how they operated. It was a good way to soak up little details about the game, including how the manager managed.

Mike Matheny, the Cardinals' skipper, walked up to me. "Hey, Mitch! What do you have today?"

"Nothing. I'm down today."

"Alright, tell you what. Gibby's looking for somebody to talk to. Go talk to him."

Gibby?

Bob Gibson?

"You want me to go talk to Bob Gibson?"

Sure enough, Gibson sat on the opposite end of the dugout, and when I approached him rather awkwardly and sat down next to him on the bench, he greeted me warmly.

"Oh, hello, Mitch!"

Really?

Bob Gibson knows my name?

We talked for at least two innings. I wish I could tell you what we talked about, but honestly, I was so incredibly star struck, I don't remember any specifics.

Some guys get this close and no closer.

Some dreams vanish right before your eyes.

Who knew whether I would get the chance to take that last step into the big leagues, but I was so close I could taste it.

9

The Call

ONE OF THE GUYS I looked up to during my minor league career was my buddy, Marco Gonzales.

Marco was the Cardinals' top draft pick in 2013, such a powerful pitcher that he jumped from Double A to St. Louis for part of the 2014 season—the first starter to make that leap in sixteen years. The Cardinals won the National League's Central Division for the second straight year, and coming out of the bullpen, Marco wound up winning two Division Series games against the Dodgers, including the clincher. Like me, he started 2015 with the Triple A Memphis Redbirds.

We often roomed together on the road, and I took every opportunity to pepper him with questions about the big-league experience.

On the morning of April 21, 2015, we were in our hotel room in Round Rock, Texas, getting ready to head to the ballpark, when the phone rang. It was our manager, Mike Shildt.

"Mitch, are you busy? You mind coming down to the lobby real quick?"

"Sure. No problem."

Putting two and two together, Marco got this big smile on his face as I walked out the door. "You're going to the big leagues!"

I wasn't so sure.

Ordinarily, somebody at the big club had to get hurt or traded before the front office could make this sort of move, and as far as I knew, no significant roster changes had taken place.

Maybe they're just giving me the night off?

When I stepped off the elevator and turned to my left, heading toward the lobby, I saw Shildt and minor league pitching coach Brian Eversgerd. We called him Gerdy.

They were both smiling, and before I could say anything, Mike started talking about my dream. "Do you remember telling stories of you being on the ship and just having the thought that you would lose your dream because you fulfilled your commitment? And wondering if you were ever going to step on a baseball field again or ever have the opportunity to fulfill that dream?"

By this point, my heart was racing. "Oh, yeah. I remember that."

"You remember laying in your rack and thinking, *What would it be like if I could fulfill that and be a big leaguer?*"

"Yeah, of course."

"You just did it. You're going to D.C. tonight."

Then he handed me a plane ticket.

I choked back tears as we hugged it out. Didn't Tom Hanks say there was no crying in baseball? It was hard to control my emotions, especially as I looked straight into the eyes of these two veteran baseball men, their eyes watering. They knew what this moment meant to me, to the Cardinals, to baseball.

I excused myself and stepped outside to call my dad, who had been visiting a hospital. He had stopped for lunch at a Chinese buffet restaurant in Chattanooga.

"Dad, are you sitting down?"

"Well, I can be."

"I'm going up!"

He didn't understand. "I'm sorry?"

Still in a state of shock, I tried to explain what had just happened and told him I was about to catch a flight to D.C. to join the Cardinals for their three-game series against the Nationals.

Nobody understood my difficult journey to this defining moment quite like my dad, who said, "Mitch, you've done good! I'm so proud of you!"

When I reached Mandi, she was sheltered in the downstairs bathroom of her townhouse in Braselton, Georgia, because her area was under a tornado warning. Soon my fiancé called her parents and fired up her laptop to book a flight to Washington for the following day. Like my parents, Mandi was determined to be there for my Major League debut.

Frankly, for me, the rest of the day was a blur.

I know I caught a flight to D.C., but I don't remember anything about it.

***

When you walk into any Major League Baseball stadium it is difficult not to feel the ghosts.

To truly love the game, you must love its history, including the colorful stories of larger-than-life characters such Babe Ruth, Ty Cobb, Roberto Clemente, Sandy Koufax, and Hank Aaron.

If you were alive to see it, surely you will never forget the day when the immortal Ted Williams walked to the plate at Fenway Park and slammed a homerun in the final at bat of his remarkable career.

Boy, did he know how to leave the stage.

How could we forget the night when Reggie Jackson became Mr. October, hitting three consecutive home runs during game six of the 1977 World Series?

Or the day when Willie Mays made the most amazing catch in the history of the storied Polo Grounds?

Or the night when Kirk Gibson, nursing two gimpy legs, stepped to the plate at Dodger Stadium, took the great Dennis Eckersley deep, and then limped around the bases?

Here's the funny thing. Except for Gibson's inspirational homer, which happened right before I turned three, and of which I have no personal memories, I wasn't around to see any of these. I didn't get to experience any of these up close or on television or in a breathless reading of the next day's newspaper. But because I love the game, because I cherish its traditions, because I see the game as something organic, lovingly passed down from one generation to the next, these moments are a part of me and always will be.

That's one of the reasons my wild ride to the St. Louis Cardinals' lineup is so meaningful to me.

It is incredibly humbling to know that I will always have a little piece of baseball history—becoming the 20,843rd person to play in a Major League game.

When I was called up, a reporter told me that I was poised to become the first Naval Academy graduate to play in the Major Leagues since Willard Roland "Nemo" Gaines.

I must admit, I didn't know the name, or anything about his story.

In time, I learned that Gaines had pitched for the Midshipmen from 1919–21, graduated from the Academy and earned his commission, and then was granted a special leave from the Navy to pitch for the Washington Senators. He appeared in four games during the 1921 season, pitching 4 2/3 innings with five hits, two walks, one strikeout, and no runs.

No other Naval Academy graduate ever made it to the Major Leagues until me—a span of ninety-four years.

Baseball is such a stats-driven sport, all those disparate eras connected by colliding digits, and I can take a measure of pride in knowing that Gaines' long-ago story will someday echo in my obituary.

But by now, you understand that my story casts a much bigger shadow.

There was a little bit of Jim Morris in me, and a little bit of Roy Hobbs too.

***

At some point, I found out about the life event that had enabled me to be called up: Outfielder Peter Bourjos' wife had just had a baby, and the Cardinals gave him three days off, which allowed them to take a chance on a Triple A relief pitcher—presumably for three days.

Late that afternoon, I walked into the visitors' clubhouse at Nationals Park. The Cardinals headed out for batting practice, and when I walked past the manager's office, with my bag on my shoulder, I spotted Mike Matheny.

Mike understood long odds.

He had been a four-time Gold Glove catcher in a thirteen-year playing career with the Milwaukee Brewers, Toronto Blue Jays, St. Louis Cardinals, and San Francisco Giants. He was one of only three catchers ever to go an entire 100-game-plus season without an error.

After hanging up his spikes, Mike actually coached Little League Baseball—and was hired to manage the Cardinals despite having no professional managing or coaching experience.

When he looked up from his notes and saw me, Mike flashed a big smile and got up to shake my hand and give me a hug. "You did it! I'm so glad you're here!"

Everything happened so fast, but then he punctuated the warm greeting with the rhetorical question that confirmed my official entrance into the pressure-cooker world of big-league baseball.

"Are you ready to go tonight?"

"Of course," I said, trying to play it cool.

Then I went off to find my locker, seeing for the first time my very own number 40 Cardinals jersey, with my name stitched onto the back.

I didn't see any action that night but was sure busy the next day. It seemed like the whole country was talking about my story, and the demand for interviews was so intense that the Cardinals' public relations department arranged a press conference for me. This made me a little uncomfortable. After all, I hadn't pitched an inning in the big leagues yet.

The enormity of my accomplishment began to sink in, and it was hard for me to believe that this wide-eyed little boy who had spent so many days firing fastballs into that imaginary concrete strike zone—pretending to be John Smoltz—had grown into a Major League player surrounded by reporters.

Then, while escorted to the media event, I spotted him, my hero, and experienced the strangest feeling.

About two years earlier, I had met Smoltz during a baseball conference at a Georgia church.

But now...

"Mitch!" Smoltz yelled out as I walked toward the media room.

Me? Is he talking to me?

I couldn't believe my idol knew my name.

"I'm so excited you're here!" he said, reaching out to shake my hand. "I'm so pumped for you!"

Smoltz was standing with Bob Costas, his partner on the television broadcast that night, who shared his enthusiasm for my story. "I'm so proud of you!"

Every rookie who makes it to the Majors has a dream, and the odds of negotiating the leap are astronomical—"long enough," Matheny said, "to make you not even want to try."

In one respect, I was just another '90s kid who had dreamed of following in the footsteps of John Smoltz. That I made it through the maze to claim the cheese was incredibly unlikely, even under the most favorable conditions.

But my story was also unique.

My five-year layoff and all it represented threw me into an entirely different category.

Many baseball people had once written me off. In the context of those five lost years—and the depressing radar digits of 2013—I showed up in the Major Leagues as something of a Lazarus figure.

"He was throwing how slow?"

"He was out of the game for how long?"

Soon, I learned that sportswriters, fans, and my own teammates were embracing my journey as an object lesson that transcended the game.

Perhaps Cardinals pitcher Lance Lynn, who became one of my good friends, said it best: My story "proved nothing's impossible if you want it bad enough."

People wanted to know how I had kept the faith for those five long years, why I hadn't given up on my dream.

Looking back on those days now, I know that's a complex question requiring a complex answer. For one thing, quitting was not in my nature, thanks in part to the lessons I learned from my dad. For another, baseball and the possibility of someday playing in the big leagues were deeply embedded in my identity. Without this hope, who was I? Chasing the dream gave me purpose, and ultimately, catching the dream made me who I am.

One element of my story cannot be minimized. All those people who told me "No" and encouraged me to forget about baseball and get on with my life? They didn't discourage me. They made me want it all the more. They filled me with a powerful resolve. They gave me something to prove. In the end, I churned those doubts into the rocket fuel that powered me into the baseball history books.

The attention I received that first week in Washington was a bit overwhelming, but in time, I learned that many baseball people had rooted for me.

"So many of us admired how he had served his country, done his duty," Matheny said. "And he had this dream that was complicated by [the fact that he] had been away from baseball for such a long time. The odds were stacked against him, but we were all pulling for him...So when he got called up, that made it a great celebration for everybody who had witnessed the progression."

It was humbling to have people talk about me as an inspirational figure, a living and breathing symbol of the power of dreaming big, overcoming obstacles, and never giving up.

"We all knew Mitch had to fight to make it to the Major Leagues," Lance Lynn said. "None of us knew all the stuff he had to go through, how tough it was."

No one knew how trapped I had felt during those five years away from the game.

No one knew about those desperate times when the woman I loved had pushed me to the edge.

No one knew about my out-of-control drinking.

No one knew I felt that God had abandoned me.

No one knew about the loaded gun.

But none of that mattered now, because I was turning my tattoo into the truth.

***

Four games into my big-league career, I was surrounded by zeros, wondering if I would make it into a game before being sent back down. It was time for Peter Bourjos, the new father, to be reactivated. Somebody had to go.

I began to understand the routine, so on the plane ride to Milwaukee for a series with the Brewers, I carefully watched as one of our utility infielders was called up to see Matheny. I knew what this meant: He was being sent back to Triple A, and I was staying in The Show. I felt bad for him, but what a relief.

Under the circumstances, it seemed logical that I would eventually be called out of the bullpen. They wanted to see what I could do. Otherwise, they wouldn't have kept me.

Several family members and friends, including Mandi and my parents, had traveled to Washington in the hopes of seeing my Major

League debut, only to be disappointed when I didn't make it into a game. Such is the life of a relief pitcher. You never know when you're going to get the call, especially when you're the unproven rookie.

In an odd twist of fate, Mandi was transitioning between jobs and had seized the opportunity to take an interview with General Electric, which had a hub in Milwaukee. Like many aspects of our life together, that sequence of events felt like it was meant to be.

Early the next morning, when Mandi showed up at The Pfister Hotel, the posh landmark in downtown Milwaukee, I was still trying to sleep off my initiation. Some of the guys had welcomed me to the big leagues on the plane from D.C. to Milwaukee, and we had quite the celebration.

"It was pretty comical, trying to explain to the people at the front desk that I was there to see my fiancé, and not realizing that they needed to be protected from people just showing up," Mandi recalled. "I didn't know anything about that world."

The word spread quickly among my friends, especially on Facebook, and several of my old buddies from the Naval Academy and the Navy started calling and texting with good wishes. Mike Alvarez, formerly operations specialist second class, who served with me on the U.S.S. Ponce, got in touch, and said he was coming to Milwaukee.

Miller Park was a long way from the Persian Gulf and those lonely nights when Alvarez and I often manned the late watch, our conversations often turning to my seemingly impossible dream.

It didn't take me long to understand that so many people who had dared to believe in me all those years before now felt like they were taking the magical ride with me. And that made it all the sweeter.

"I was just so proud of Mitch for fighting so hard to make his dream come true," Alvarez said. "And I had to be there to see it in person."

For the second game of the series on April 25, I arranged for tickets for Mike and three of his friends, and they wound up sitting next to Mandi, who was a bundle of nerves. "I was just trying to hide," she said.

Two years after he worried that I might be deluding myself, while clinging to the lowest rung of professional baseball, Mark McCoy had driven from his home in New Jersey to Washington, hoping I would get into a game against the Nationals. When I didn't see action, he had to drive home. Determined to see my debut, one way or another, he bought the MLB television package.

Four days later, he sat in his living room, watching the St. Louis-Milwaukee game. Would tonight be the night?

"I was so happy to be wrong about him being a PR stunt," McCoy said. "Mitch battled so hard and earned everything he got, and I was so proud of him, happy for him."

With our ace, Adam Wainwright, starting, I figured I would have to wait another day at least. Waino would go his usual seven innings, and one of our setup guys would take over and eventually give way to closer Trevor Rosenthal.

We were leading 2-0 in the top of the fifth when Wainwright popped out to first. While running it out, he tumbled to the ground. Only later would we learn that he had snapped his Achilles tendon. What a bad break. He was out for the year.

Within a few moments, the bullpen phone rang, and the pitching coach looked at me. "Mitch, get loose."

This was the call I had waited for my whole life, and it felt like my heart was going to explode as I stepped to the rubber and started warming up.

Several minutes later, when I headed for the fence and the security guard opened the gate, I looked up at the massive crowd. That's when it hit me. All those people were looking right at me.

The Cardinals travel well, so when the public address announcer called my name, the St. Louis fans roared. Many of them already knew my name. Many knew about my unlikely road to this defining moment. Many saw me as a symbol. They weren't just cheering for me. They were cheering for the possibility of someone like me, and what it said about America. They were cheering for the power of dreaming big and making those dreams come true.

Just then, my old buddy Alvarez was standing in line to get a beer.

"Got goosebumps when I heard them call Mitch's name," he said. "Sort of said to myself, 'Screw the beer!' and ran back to my seat."

Soon, he and Mandi were hugging and crying.

"I was so happy for Mitch because I knew how hard he had worked to get to that point," Mandi said, "but I didn't understand the magnitude of the achievement. Not then. I just knew I was so proud of him."

Unfortunately, my parents had just boarded a flight from Atlanta to Chattanooga. Just as they learned that I was entering the game, the flight attendant insisted they turn off their phones. "Pretty frustrating and pretty unfortunate timing," Dad would say later.

Feeling the need to share, Mom turned to the stranger sitting next to her. "I know we're being loud, but my son just entered his first Major League game, and we don't know what's going on..."

"He did?"

She started telling the man my life story. Suddenly, I had a new fan at 35,000 feet.

Back at Miller Park, my world turned surreal and muscle memory took over, as the stadium noise faded and I headed for the zone against first baseman Adam Lind.

Slightly more than three years after my dramatically diminished velocity gave many people pause about my future, I stepped onto the mound full of confidence and determined to bring the heat.

Recalling the scene, teammate Matt Adams said: "It was a pretty cool moment... The confidence that Mitch brought to the mound, you could just feel it. He'd been preparing for that opportunity for a long time and he was getting those guys out."

No place for distractions.

No room for doubt.

Whoosh.

Fastball, clocking 95 miles per hour, right over the plate. Strike one.

Fastball, registering 96, in the same neighborhood. Strike two.

After he fouled one off, I threw a cutter, and Lind swung over the top of it, striking out, and I felt a satisfaction I had been chasing my entire life.

My tattoo was now the truth, and the view from the summit was something to behold.

10

Success with a Shadow

Jason Simontacchi was on a bus.

At the time, he was the pitching coach for the Springfield Cardinals, and they were on the road, driving late into the night.

Someone texted him with a link about my first game, and after devouring the details, he handed his smart phone to one of the guys across the aisle.

"How freaking awesome is this!"

With the game televised live by both the Cardinals' syndication network as well as the Brewers', my Major League debut was seen by a large crowd of baseball fans across the Midwest. Mark McCoy was one of many across the country who used the MLB.TV package to watch the game.

My story received prominent mention on ESPN's *SportsCenter*, and newspapers and websites reported extensively on the achievement.

After pitching 1 1/3 scoreless innings—giving up two hits and two walks after my first strikeout—I was replaced by Matt Belisle, who got the 5-3 Cardinals win.

Matheny credited me with doing "a real nice job."

"He came in and did exactly what we hoped he would do."

Victor Nunez was stationed in Japan.

When he heard the news, Victor's mind flashed back to all those days on the flight deck aboard the USS Ponce, when our floating game of catch on the high seas kept my dream alive, in my head as well as in my arm.

"I was so proud of Mitch," he said. "I just remember thinking, *Wow! He really did it. He went through all that time away, worked incredibly hard, and achieved his dream.* I felt like I had a little piece of the dream myself."

The crush of media around me after the game was overwhelming, and all of the reporters wanted to know how it felt to finally get out on the field and throw in a big-league game.

Maybe you think that because I had dreamed so long, worked so hard, fantasized so intently on every little detail, that the reality would not live up to the vibrant picture in my mind.

Actually, it was everything I had dreamed about and more.

Standing on the mound, completely confident in my skills, feeling the pressure to perform, I knew I was born for that situation. It felt right.

Twenty-three years is a long time to keep a flame burning bright in your heart, but the battle was worth it, just to have that feeling for a few precious moments.

I knew I wasn't alone.

All across America and beyond, a small cadre of friends and fans were taking this ride with me. People I had never met were celebrating the culmination of my long journey out of the shadows, and it was a warm and humbling feeling to be smothered with such love.

"There are a lot of people involved in this story," I told a reporter from MLB.com. "My name is on the front of it, but there are a lot of people who have helped me get to where I'm at through struggles and the years where we weren't sure it was going to happen."

While strapped in on his bus, Simontacchi flashed back to the day he met me at spring training.

In those days, he knew I was the longest of shots but still, he urged patience, a wise prescription. I thought time was my enemy, but it was never so simple, and Simontacchi was one of several coaches who helped propel me toward the big leagues.

"To see how far Mitch came and how he struggled against various challenges...it was just so inspiring," Simontacchi said. "Here's a guy who served his country, did his duty, and the odds are stacked incredibly high against him ever getting to play in the majors. What a testament to the power of tenacity."

Perhaps no one had shown more faith in me or played a bigger role in my comeback than Brent Strom, who by then had moved on to become pitching coach for the Houston Astros. While in Oakland for a game with the Athletics, Strom was in his hotel room and watched the televised highlights of me in a Cardinals uniform, striking out the first man I faced.

"I was just very, very proud of him, as everyone who was involved with that guy should be," he said.

The crowd in Milwaukee included Captain Tim Crone, my former CO, one of several Navy colleagues who had helped me and cheered for me on the long road from Annapolis.

Captain Patrick Kulokowski saw the news a day or two later on Facebook, which led him to google for other articles. He reached out to offer his congratulations.

"Mitch did it the right way, and I was just so happy for him, that he kept plugging and worked through all those obstacles," he said.

The big hug and kiss from Mandi outside the visitors' clubhouse after the game was extra sweet, and soon I learned that my parents had seen a video clip of my first strike-out after landing in Chattanooga.

Because they knew what others didn't, it was an especially emotional moment for Cindy and Cy. The triumphant image of their boy finally achieving his dream on live TV filled up their world.

"Mitch just never quit," Mom said. "He just never quit believing. At some point, just to save my sanity, I quit hoping. All the rejection started to take a toll on me. But Mitch? He never quit."

***

My initiation into the Major Leagues happened during a road trip to Cleveland.

After all, you're nobody until the other team's fans mercilessly harass you.

In early May, I was warming up in the bullpen at Progressive Field, trying to block out the hostile atmosphere.

At this point, I was still adjusting to the whole big-league experience, including all of the first-class accommodations that contrasted so dramatically with the minors, the big crowds, the media attention, the pressure to win.

For some reason, one rather obnoxious Indians fan started taunting me.

He was pretty nasty and relentless.

On and on this guy went, trying to get into my head, but I just kept working through my routine and hitting the catcher's target.

Welcome to the big leagues, Mitch.

This sort of abuse is part of the game, and you learn not to take it personally.

After a few minutes, the guy stopped his yapping.

He had pulled out his phone and googled me.

"Hey, L-T," he finally yelled out. "Sorry about that! I didn't know your background..."

He said something about being former enlisted, and that he appreciated my service.

"You're alright with me!"

One of my new teammates, veteran left-handed reliever Randy Choate, stood nearby, closely watching this scene. He started laughing.

A few minutes later, another Cleveland fan in the same section started popping off at me.

"No, man, stop it," the first fan insisted. "He served. He's good. He's cool."

It was all pretty amusing, certainly the first time someone had ever apologized for giving me grief.

The military angle was deeply embedded in my story as a Major League rookie. All the media attention humbled me, and as expected, my success gave the Naval Academy and the Navy a jolt of positive publicity.

"For all we do in terms of recognizing returning veterans," Baseball Commissioner Rob Manfred said, "it's such a remarkable story for him to come back and play."

My Navy service helped me bond with several of my teammates, especially with my manager, who also had two grandfathers who had served as part of the Greatest Generation. Like me, he was a patriotic guy who felt something stir deep inside when he heard the National Anthem before every game.

But ultimately, my story didn't matter unless I could do the job.

All that mattered was my ability to throw strikes.

"Mitch was super focused on becoming an effective big-league pitcher," said All-Star right-hander Lance Lynn.

After all those years away from the game, I was determined to make the most of my opportunity.

"Mitch came in with a very business-like attitude," Matheny said. "He had the discipline and the toughness."

Of course, if that shining moment in Milwaukee had been all I got, if that inning-and-a-third was the extent of my big-league career? If that single line in the box score was the sum total of my contribution to Cardinals' history? Honestly, that would have been enough. It would have been enough for the wide-eyed little boy who still lived inside me. It would have been enough for the Naval officer who desperately needed to prove all those doubters wrong.

Achieving my dream after all those years was incredibly gratifying.

It could have been one out or fifteen years. Didn't matter.

I was a big leaguer, now and forever. Nobody could ever take that away from me.

But fortunately, Milwaukee was just the start of my magic carpet ride through 2015, and the second milestone of my Major League career was nearly as memorable as the first.

***

The Cardinals were in the middle of an eight-game winning streak when we traveled to Chicago for a series with the Cubs at storied Wrigley Field.

The game went back and forth, we took the lead, and I pitched a scoreless sixth inning to grab my first win.

Wow, what a feeling.

After the game, I got Matheny and my teammates to sign the score-card, which remains a treasured keepsake.

After about a month with the Cardinals, we were on a flight some-where, and one of the guys approached my seat and whispered, "Skip-per wants to see you!"

In my mind, I flashed back to the first time I had heard this phrase on an airplane.

Now it was my turn: I was the low man on the totem pole in the bullpen.

Now the manager wanted to have a conversation with me at 34,000 feet.

"Mitch," he said, "you're doing everything right. But we need a guy with a hot bat..."

The Cardinals were sending me down.

Walking back to my seat, I wasn't sure what this meant for my career. Maybe this was it? Maybe this little taste of the big leagues was all I would ever get?

However, one thing Matheny said had encouraged me: "Stay ready! Keep doing what you're doing, and you'll get a shot."

By this point, I began to understand how hard it is to stay in the big leagues, and especially since the Cardinals had so little invested in me, I would have to fight and be very fortunate to get back.

"I remember talking to Mitch and telling him not to get discour-aged," Lance Lynn said. "'This is how baseball works. Stay positive, keep working hard. Don't let it beat you down.'"

Several weeks later, they called me back, and I would spend the rest of the 2015 season bouncing between St. Louis and Triple A Memphis, negotiating the roster dance all too familiar to Major League rookies.

"Mitch got a chance to show us what he could do, and he made the most of the opportunity," Matheny said. "He pitched well."

By any measure, my 2015 season was solid, with twenty-six appear-ances, a 2-1 record, and a 3.67 ERA. During one stretch, I made nine straight appearances (a total of ten innings) without giving up a run.

It didn't take me long to understand that my body reacted differently to the Major League experience.

Adrenaline pumps much harder when you suddenly find yourself pitching in front of 40,000 fans and many more on television. There's more torque on your body, and that means more strain on your arm.

Toward the end of the season, my right arm began to feel the strain. The outside of my forearm became sore, and when I finished throwing, my tricep was sore too, almost tender to the touch.

Never before in my competitive career had I experienced any issues with my arm. This was completely new territory, and I just assumed that this nagging condition was part of pitching in the bigs, something that I needed to live with. I was still getting good rotation, and my velocity was still in the mid-90s.

In September, the Cardinals qualified for the playoffs, and while I didn't expect to make the twenty-five-man postseason roster, I was beyond excited for our last series of the year, in Atlanta against the Braves.

You know where I came from and the dream that powered me all the way from that driveway in Lawrenceville, fantasizing about pitching for the Braves.

How special it would be to get into a game at Turner Field.

It seemed like everybody I knew within a 200-mile radius wanted to be there, and I had arranged for at least twenty-five tickets.

But when Matheny found out about my soreness, he called me into his clubhouse office.

"You're battling something, and I'm not gonna throw you," he said. "Let's get it checked out, so you can be ready for next season."

This was incredibly disappointing for me as well as all my friends and family, but it was hard for me to argue with Matheny's time-worn wisdom.

I was a Cardinal now and needed to be smart with my body.

Next year, I would be back, good as new.

11

Victory Redefined

WHEN MANDI AND I decided to get married, we agreed that the ceremony needed to take place in the sweet spot, after baseball season and before spring training.

She had settled into her career with General Electric and lived on the north side of Atlanta as I shuttled between St. Louis and Memphis, so it made sense to hold the ceremony in Georgia, near most of our family and friends. She found this cool farm in Watkinsville, where we exchanged vows before a big crowd in an open-air building on November 21, 2015. It was a fun setting, the opposite of stuffy, with the reception featuring several different buffet tables of fancy Southern food and kids of all ages playing cornhole.

During this period, my pitching arm still felt a little sore and sensitive. If I slept on it wrong, especially if I unconsciously stretched it above my head during the night, it would start barking, as we say in baseball. But I tried to put what I believed to be an occasional nuisance out of my mind, determined to enjoy the time off with my new wife before spring training beckoned.

I was a Cardinal now, and they were counting on me to rest up and get ready to rock.

At the end of the 2015 season, I felt great about what I had accomplished and excited about 2016.

Who knew how many years I would get out of my aging body, but I was determined to enjoy the ride as long as it lasted.

When you make it to the big leagues, you don't assume you'll stay. Not at all. But you come to battle a nagging thought: *Well, I'm here. Why would I not be able to come back?*

Guys will tell you that they tried to stay in the bigs the best they could, understanding the intense competition with all those gifted athletes pushing hard to make their own mark in a world of finite jobs.

There's room for humility in that pressure-packed world, but there's also the pounding need for a certain defiance.

They were going to have to pry that Cardinals jersey off my back.

I was going to work my tail off and do whatever it took to stay in the big leagues.

Soon after I arrived in Jupiter in February 2016, with a coveted position on the forty-man roster, my arm began barking even louder. The time away from throwing had not helped.

Several days before the pitcher-catcher report date, I began my personal workouts at the Cardinals' facility. From the first throw on the mound, I knew something was wrong. It was a different sort of pain—"on the inside aspect of the elbow," recalled team orthopedic surgeon Dr. George Paletta.

"In the late times of the acceleration phase, when he had the ball in his hand and was just about to accelerate, he would have pain in the medial aspect of the elbow," Paletta said.

The medical team brought me in for an MRI, and everything looked normal. No apparent ligament tear.

Then they started putting me through neurological tests. No nerve damage.

Eventually, the Cardinals sent me to Gulf Breeze in the Florida panhandle to see Dr. James Andrews, the renowned orthopedic surgeon, the third doctor to examine me.

Well known for his work with high-profile athletes including Bo Jackson, Roger Clemons, and John Smoltz, Andrews put my elbow through a stress test, simulating the pitching motion, during an MRI. This enabled him to see that my ulnar collateral ligament (UCL) was partially detached from the bone.

The UCL is necessary to stabilize the inner elbow when you throw a baseball.

No wonder I was feeling such distress. The pain blared like a siren inside my body.

"You're going to have to have surgery," Andrews said.

In the old days, a pitcher's career was over when he tore his UCL.

That all changed in 1974, when Dr. Frank Jobe performed ligament replacement surgery on Los Angeles Dodgers pitcher Tommy John. At the time, it was considered an experimental procedure, and no one could say for sure whether an arm repaired in such a manner would hold up to the various stresses of pitching a baseball.

But after sitting out for nearly two full seasons, John returned to the lineup as good as new, helping lead the Dodgers to back-to-back World Series appearances in 1977–78. He would pitch another fourteen years and make the All-Star team three more times as the so-called Tommy John surgery became a routine part of baseball, a lifeline for guys like me.

Soon, I learned that I was also a candidate for a different remedy.

Tommy John requires harvesting a tendon from another area of the patient's body and then transplanting it into the elbow, to act as a replacement for the UCL.

Andrews started telling me about this new kind of surgery, which he and others had performed many times on younger athletes.

Because I had pitched a relatively small number of innings in the big leagues, he concluded that my UCL was still in relatively good shape: detached but apparently not frayed or severely damaged.

"You're in that small window of pro athletes who qualify for the new surgery," he said.

After consulting with Paletta, Andrews told me that he thought they could bypass Tommy John and instead use the new procedure—called a primary repair—to fix my existing UCL.

"There's no way to say for certain until we get in there," Andrews said.

Had my five-year layoff and then my furious race to get my arm back into shape contributed to my injury?

It takes time to strengthen a ligament for the sort of stress required to throw a baseball with the force required in the pro game, and I couldn't deny the reality that I had negotiated a steep mountain in a short amount of time.

No one could say with any certainty whether the abrupt pattern of inactivity and stress had caused my ligament to detach—whether chasing my dream so vigorously had ultimately endangered it—but Andrews saw a clear linkage and suggested that, under the circumstances, the injury may have been inevitable.

"If I tell a sprinter to go do a sprint and then I tell him to sit for fifteen minutes, and then come back and do another sprint, the chances of him pulling something or tearing something are pretty high," he explained. "If they don't warm up or stay loose, they're gonna get hurt. You played baseball your whole life, and then you took five years off. Then you went to the highest level in two years. That's how you tore it. It just came off the bone."

Andrews turned me over to Paletta, a skilled and widely acclaimed surgeon who prepped me for both operations at his Missouri clinic on June 14, 2016.

If he determined that the UCL was not in good enough shape to reattach, he would perform Tommy John. While routine and usually successful, it required a longer period of rehabilitation.

"If Mitch had had the Tommy John reconstruction, that recovery is somewhere in the order of twelve to sixteen months," Paletta said. "So, he was looking at missing potentially most of two seasons."

At that point in my life, two seasons felt like a lifetime.

No one could say if my aging body had two seasons to waste. We all knew we were racing the clock.

The doctors believed I could make it back in seven to eight months with the primary repair, which meant I could potentially be ready to pitch at the start of the 2017 season.

Still, all the parties agreed that Paletta would make the decision between Tommy John and primary repair in the operating room—after he opened up my elbow and sized up the extent of my injury.

"Based on the pattern of the tear...directly off the bone," he determined that the primary repair would work, and carefully repaired my UCL.

When I woke up in recovery and saw that they hadn't harvested a strip from my hamstring, I was told that I had become the first Major League pitcher to undergo the primary repair procedure.

About two months later, Kansas City Royals right-hander Seth Maness, my former Cardinals teammate, faced a similar situation—and opted for the same surgery, also performed by Paletta.

Writing about his comeback, the Associated Press played up the experimental nature of the operation and lauded him as "a willing guinea pig."

"Years from now," the AP speculated, "they may call it the 'Seth Maness' surgery."

Sometimes, you just have to laugh and shake your head.

Literally being on the cutting edge didn't land me in the history books, but it kept me in the game.

By the time Maness went under the knife, I was two months into my scheduled rehab in Jupiter, often going through treatments alongside Lance Lynn, who was recovering from Tommy John surgery.

"Mitch was very determined, and he worked very hard," Lynn said. "He was going to do whatever he could to come back."

The program for Tommy John was well-established, thanks to decades of trial-and-error, but with this new surgery, which produced a new set of challenges, we were all flying a bit blind, struggling to devise the right path to recovery. What sort of treatments? How many months? Maness wasn't the only guinea pig, and at times, it was frustrating to be chasing something not knowing whether it would disappear right in front of my eyes.

In the lonely moments, trying to stay motivated, I sometimes flashed back to those quiet nights at sea, when I desperately held on to the idea of playing professional baseball.

Now other people doubted me, for different reasons, and I drew strength from their skepticism.

The next spring, the Cardinals reactivated me, and I participated in Major League spring training. When they sent me to Memphis, I wasn't 100 percent. But now more than ever, I was a man in a hurry, a man who wanted to make the guys in St. Louis believe in me and call me back to the rubber at Busch Stadium. Now more than ever, I could feel my time slipping away, so I pushed through the discomfort, trying to ignore the signals that my body was sending.

My velocity was decent, consistently in the low-90s, and it was reasonable to assume I could get it back up to full speed. But especially when throwing the combination of the cutter and the fastball, my forearm sometimes exploded in pain.

No one could pinpoint why this was happening, because my elbow felt great.

Twice in a span of nine days, they placed me on the disabled list.

Every time I tried to throw, my body kept failing me.

Part of me was dying. I could feel it.

In late April, while on a road trip, once again, my forearm began aching terribly, rendering me unable to effectively control the ball. The Redbirds placed me on the DL for the third time in that young season, and a wave of resignation washed over me.

This is it.

I think I'm done.

The guys around the clubhouse could sense the change in me as I packed up my stuff and walked out the door, headed for extended rehab in Jupiter.

Getting well was now my job, and it was getting old.

Baseball is a heartless business with no room for sentimentality. Sooner or later, we all arrive at the same place, and rarely are endings happy.

About two weeks after arriving in Jupiter, on May 9, 2017, I walked into the clubhouse in my street clothes, and one of the minor league front office guys told me Gary LaRocque, the farm system director, wanted to see me in his upstairs office.

I suspected what this meant, but it still stung when he told me the Cardinals were releasing me.

It had been less than eleven months since my successful surgery, and we still hadn't figured out what was going on with my forearm.

It was not lost on me that if I had undergone Tommy John, I would still have been in rehab from the surgery at that point, without the pressure of anything other than getting well. So, it was hard for me not to feel that I was being punished for trying to do right by the Cardinals and get back to action sooner.

As the initial shock and anger wore off, I was able to see the situation from the organization's vantage point. The Cardinals had just paid me an entire year's big-league salary of more than $500,000 without getting a single inning out of me in a St. Louis uniform. This wasn't my fault, but it wasn't theirs either. Injuries happen. Bodies wear out. I was a thirty-one-year-old guy with a sore arm coming off experimental surgery, and in a world loaded with hot young prospects with healthy bodies, it didn't make much business sense to keep throwing money at me.

In the next couple of months, I kept trying to push my arm back into shape, with mixed results and no real answers, and worked out for the Orioles and the Cubs. But nobody wanted me.

Did it hurt, all that rejection? Of course. I'm not going to lie. It was devastating.

Sure, I wish my time in the sun had lasted longer, but now I know that every moment was a precious gift.

My time in the bigs will always feel especially sweet to me because I had to fight so hard for it.

The competitor in me will always wonder what might have been, if I had been able to play longer, the career I might have enjoyed under different circumstances.

The competitor in me will always remember that when the Cardinals won the World Series without me in 2011—beating the Texas Rangers in seven games—I was on the U.S.S. Carr somewhere in the South Atlantic, fulfilling my commitment and dealing with the consequences of a failing marriage.

But I'm so proud of the one year I had.

That one year was everything. It was enough to last me for the rest of my life.

I had achieved my dream, and no one could ever take it away from me.

But now it was over, and I had to figure out what to do with the rest of my life.

***

When the Cardinals cut me, Mandi and I had been living in the Jupiter area for nearly a year. She had quit her job after getting pregnant, and our daughter Rylan was born in November 2016.

We went six months without any income, and the bank account began to dwindle. Somebody probably would have given me a shot to slog through the minors all over again, with little hope of anything more, but this thought depressed me, especially knowing that such a scenario would require me to drag Mandi and little Rylan across the country, from one town to the next, in a desperate attempt to cling to something that was quickly slipping beyond my grasp. I loved the game but didn't want to be *that* guy.

After giving my agent ample time to scare up any serious interest without getting a nibble, I officially announced my retirement on Twitter, knowing that I had given baseball everything I had—and then started planning for the next chapter.

Toward the end of the year, we found out that Mandi was pregnant with our second child, which increased my urgency to move on and find a new career. My son Camden would be born in June 2018.

Fortunately, I had a Naval Academy degree to fall back on and plenty of options.

After we moved back to the Atlanta area, where we had bought a home and Mandi landed a good job, I diligently connected with various friends and colleagues, researching career opportunities.

One day, I called John Mozeliak, the general manager of the Cardinals. Mo and I had a good relationship, and I knew he would shoot straight with me. Because I loved baseball, we discussed the possibility of some sort of front office job with the organization, but he made it clear that this route had its own obstacles, probably requiring a long and unpredictable rollercoaster ride through the farm system and, at first, wouldn't pay very well.

During our conversation, as he tried to give me some friendly advice, he asked, "Have you thought about something in the financial industry?"

As a matter of fact, the thought of becoming a financial advisor had been on my radar, especially because I had seen so many of my teammates and other players make such devastating mistakes despite earning big salaries.

"I think more people like you are needed in that industry," he said, which encouraged me, and the wheels started turning in my head.

After taking time to research various firms, the consensus opinion was a particular larger firm that had the best training. One thing led to another, and in September 2017, I placed a call to the local office: "I want a job. What do I do?"

I started out in the advisor training program while studying for the Series 7 and Series 66 exams, and also later obtained my insurance license.

All these years later, as an Atlanta-based financial advisor, I absolutely love my job.

Nothing will ever approach the adrenaline rush of jogging into the middle of a massive stadium, surrounded by a big crowd of cheering and jeering fans, and striking a batter out. But I have learned to chase different kinds of thrills.

It gives me genuine satisfaction to have one of my clients put their faith in me and ask me for financial advice, and then help them navigate the often-confusing investment landscape.

Every one of my clients has one or more dreams they want to achieve, while facing various challenges.

It doesn't take them long to figure out that I know a thing or two about dreaming big.

***

The Navy and the Cardinals will always be a part of me.

These two great American institutions are deeply imbedded in my soul.

In September 2024, when I returned to the Naval Academy to lead a youth baseball camp sponsored by the Major League Baseball Alumni

Association, it was impossible to escape the emotion spinning through my mind.

Talk about a full circle moment.

Walking around the Navy baseball field in my Cardinals uniform was a little surreal—my two worlds colliding for a good cause.

The Academy was a crucible that shaped me—not just into a nautical warrior but also into a disciplined individual who sets high standards for myself and pushes for excellence.

Even as the Navy fought to keep me, the lessons I learned at the Academy and in the fleet hardened me for my long battle to storm the gates of the Major Leagues.

In January 2025, I was honored to be included among the small group of athletes—one-time teammate Matt Adams and current players Alec Burleson, Luken Baker, and Jimmy Crooks—featured on the annual Cardinals Caravan, a three-day bus tour that made stops in Jefferson City, Columbia, and Hannibal, Missouri, as well as Fort Leonard Wood.

Once a Cardinal, always a Cardinal.

Being able to personally interact with fans and have the opportunity to thank them for supporting the franchise was very rewarding.

Some fans knew all about my story and came prepared to ask insightful questions.

Others were too young to have seen me play but wanted to know all about my seven-year journey to St. Louis.

On our stop at Fort Leonard Wood, members of the 22nd Marine Expeditionary Unit were shocked when I told them about sailing off to the Persian Gulf with their famed battalion on the U.S.S. Ponce.

"I'm one of you guys," I said proudly, as they gave me one of their prized challenge coins.

They didn't realize it was possible for a Navy man to make it all the way to the majors.

"Yeah," I said with a big smile. "Anything's possible."

***

My old buddy Victor Nunez is a great American success story.

Immigrating from the Dominican Republic at the age of sixteen was filled with many challenges, including the language barrier. He didn't speak English well when he moved with his family to Brooklyn. But Victor had his own dreams, and he worked hard and pursued excellence in the Navy.

Over the last two plus decades, he has carved out a long and successful career, becoming a master chief on the aircraft carrier U.S.S. Ronald Reagan.

It was gratifying to learn that Victor has made a habit of telling his young sailors my story.

"There was this guy named Mitch Harris..."

At this point, he often pulls out my old Cardinals baseball card from his wallet and launches into my unlikely journey.

"As I tell the story, some of those guys...you can see it in their eyes...they just can't believe [what I'm telling them]," Nunez said. "Mitch's story is so inspirational. So many of my sailors, they have a dream, like going to college, but it's hard work that we have to do on the ship... and it's easy to lose sight of the big picture. I like to tell them: 'If Mitch can do what he did, overcome all those odds, while staying focused on doing his job, you can too.'"

Mark McCoy now coaches high school baseball in South Florida, and he often uses me as an example for his athletes, emphasizing the importance of aiming high and never giving up.

"I know several pitchers who had better arms than Mitch but never made it to the big leagues," he said, "but I always tell my guys, 'It takes more than talent. It takes something special like Mitch had, that drive, that tenacity...'

"I personally witnessed one of the craziest stories in baseball history...this guy who never gave up on his dream, put his head down and did what he had to do, didn't become cynical or jaded...didn't give up...didn't listen when people doubted him...and achieved something that the rest of us just dream about."

***

All these years after Mandi finally picked up the phone and gave me a second chance, I can't imagine my life without her. She has made me stronger and hopefully wiser, and we have built a wonderful life with our children in suburban Atlanta, surrounded by loving and supportive relatives and friends and deeply involved in our church.

We are raising our children much in the way we were raised: to believe in God, to treat people right, and to see America as a place where anything is possible if you are willing to dream big and work hard.

When they are old enough, I intend to teach Rylan and Camden all about my unlikely baseball journey.

Not just the glory.

But also the hardship.

I want them to understand that it's perfectly acceptable to reach for something that other people tell you is impossible.

I want them to know that it's okay to have your heart broken once in a while.

I want them to know that many wonderful things are possible if you are willing to fight for your dreams.

Obviously, I hope my son Cam loves baseball as much as I do.

Recently, I began coaching his youth team, and the experience has been filled with joy and laughter.

Taking him out to our backyard and teaching him the fundamentals of catching and throwing has been a nostalgic journey, animated by visions of my six-year-old self.

When contemplating my elbow surgery and its aftermath, I worried that something might go wrong and cripple my right arm, leaving me unable to continue this ritual with my future son. These days, I don't throw the ball very hard, and I sure don't want to see my radar digits. But to my little man, I'm a hero, and that's all that matters.

For Christmas, we bought him one of those nets that returns the ball to you, and sometimes we will stay out there way past dark, catching and pitching even after Mom turns on the outside lights.

Maybe one day years from now, Cam will fire one in there, and I'll decide I can't catch my son anymore. If that happens, I'm sure I will flash back to that pivotal moment with my own father, tucked carefully into the treasure chest of my mind. The cycle of life can be bittersweet, but this will be fine and good, the way it's supposed to be.

Epilogue

By now, you understand my baseball obsession.

But you know what?

This book was also something that I was driven to do.

If you wonder why I have been so candid about my struggles on the way to the Major Leagues, why I have opened up my heart, it is because I believe we all spend too much time wallowing around in fantasyland.

Too many of us live our lives through the prism of social media, buying into the myth of perfection.

Look at that person!

He has it so great!

Why don't I have that big house?

Why don't I get to take those lavish vacations?

Why isn't my life perfect like Johnny's?

The cyber insecurity and jealousy this breeds is damaging American society, and besides, it's built on a completely false premise.

Nobody has a perfect life.

Of course, it isn't just social media that pushes a distorted view of reality. It's engrained in our culture, especially as men, to hide our scars and our failures, but the reality is that most people who have achieved any sort of success have had to deal with adversity and heartbreak.

Only later do we fully appreciate that the struggle makes the prize even more precious.

Strip away the glitter associated with playing in the big leagues, and I'm probably a guy a lot like you or your husband or your brother or your son.

Lord knows, my life is not perfect.

I've dreamed big and achieved something meaningful, but along the way, my heart was shattered into little pieces—because I dared to point my nose toward the mountaintop.

Too many people seem to believe that some of their neighbors got lucky on the way to the big job or that their route to the top was somehow negotiated without meaningful effort.

The truth is that life is hard.

If you push yourself toward the limits of your potential, beyond what is easy, beyond what is safe, you will face adversity. You will fail. You will collide with tragedy. You will get your heart broken.

But it's how you face hardship that determines who you are.

Perhaps you have an aspiration burning inside you that others doubt and even ridicule.

Perhaps someone has insisted that your dream is impossible.

It is my sincere hope that you will take inspiration out of my story, including these six defining lessons:

Your scars are beautiful.

As men, we like to reveal our battle scars because they reflect how tough we are. "Look what I survived!"

But in most cases, we don't like to talk about the wounds that created the scars—and especially our emotional scars—because society has conditioned us to avoid showing vulnerability and weakness.

By doing this, I think we are missing the point.

We should actually do the opposite: embrace the power of our scars, not as ugly reminders of endured pain but as a beautiful manifestation of healing—imperfections that allow us to understand how far we've come and what we've overcome, in the mosaic of the divine plan.

Pain isn't something to hide. It is something to understand and even celebrate.

We need to talk about what we've had to face, how we've had to struggle, because battling and ultimately transcending adversity is who you are. You are not some airbrushed version of reality, staring out from a social media page. You are the sum of your well-earned scars and the lessons they reflect.

If we don't talk through these sorts of struggles in an authentic way and model them as examples of real life, then how is the next person ever going to understand the imperative to fight and persevere?

The Bible tells us, "Iron sharpens iron" (Proverbs 27:17).

We can make each other stronger by sharing.

It can be so empowering for someone who is struggling through adversity to hear from others who've been through the fire that you can survive and ultimately triumph through tough times.

Where there are valleys, there are mountaintops.

As a pastor friend once reminded me, we often feel, as we travel through the depths of our existence, that there is no way out, no way to win. But valleys are always surrounded by mountaintops. Valleys can't exist without two mountains.

Just as the topographic contrast gives the world definition, so too must we experience the valleys in life to truly appreciate the summits we ultimately achieve.

When I look back on the lowest days of my life, especially the night when I walked into the darkness with a loaded gun, I can vividly remember the pain assaulting the man I once was. But now that pain has been churned into strength and satisfaction, the valley given context by the view from the summit.

Knowing that I will face other challenges, I now am fortified by the realization that I have the ability to climb out of the depths.

God wants us to understand that no matter how bad the situation is, you can overcome it. It takes courage and strength—and to surrender to His will—to negotiate that climb.

Embrace the dash.

One of the most universal lessons of life is carved into every tombstone.

There's the date you were born and the date you died.

In between there's a dash—the sum of your earthly existence reduced to one little horizontal line.

Are you making the most of your dash?

In the military, two time-honored songs loom large, loaded with symbolism.

"Reveille" announces the start of a new day. It demands that every military person jump out of bed with purpose.

"Taps" is played at the end of the day and also, solemnly, at the end of a warrior's life. It is a subtle reminder to all that life is precious and fleeting.

Often, we hear wake-up calls in our lives.

A little voice in your head reminds you that you need to do something important or call someone, or that you need to stop falling into certain self-destructive behaviors.

This happens to me all the time, and I believe it is God's way of speaking to me.

But it is so easy to hit the metaphorical snooze button.

Somehow, we often think we can hide from the wake-up call or put it off, but this can be a life-altering mistake.

Every day, you will face some sort of challenge, perhaps involving your family, job, faith, or friends. But don't dread the day. You have breath in your lungs. Embrace the possibility to become a better version of yourself.

Every day, you face a bugle call, and it is up to you to make the day count—because there are only so many "Reveilles" in the dash.

Understand the difference between impossible and improbable.

"Impossible" is a powerful word, and many people throw it around without understanding that few things in life are truly impossible.

Once scientists believed it was impossible to break the sound barrier in an aircraft.

Once scientists believed it was impossible to split the atom.

But these very learned people were ultimately proven wrong, and now supersonic jets and atomic energy are fundamental pillars of modern life.

Many things are improbable.

As a pastor friend once explained, "That means there's hope."

When I think back on my story, many times well-meaning people would say, "That's a cool dream but you know that's impossible, right?"

Usually, I would politely admit that perhaps it was improbable—but not impossible.

If you feel compelled to fight when the odds are stacked against you, be sure to understand the difference between these two words.

Carefully consider the risks you will take and the price you may have to pay to chase a difficult and perhaps unprecedented dream. Others may doubt you.

But never let anyone use "impossible" as a weapon to extinguish your burning ambition.

Embrace your Superman, not your Clark Kent.

During the transition from my military career to my baseball career, I struggled with my identity. It took me a while to adjust to the new reality of my new uniform.

One day, while talking to a teammate, he said, "Man, I feel like Superman when I get out there on the field. I feel invincible. I've worked so hard to be one of the best of the best. But man, when I step off that field, I feel like Clark Kent."

This thought immediately resonated with me, and I said, "So, what's the most important thing to you, in your life?"

He didn't hesitate. "My family."

"Then why," I asked, "are you giving them Clark Kent and not Superman?"

I might as well have asked myself the same question because I also struggled with this dilemma.

As an athlete, you are often revered and seen as some sort of super-human being. To achieve on the field of play, you have to embrace such a mindset because this heightened demand for excellence is deeply connected to competing and winning.

We give people who don't even know us Superman, but too often, around the people who matter the most, we revert to someone ordinary like Clark Kent.

I still feel the need to remind myself not to put all my greatest efforts into my work while rendering some lesser version of myself to my family.

It's important to understand that we have a choice. You can embrace your inner Superman in all aspects of your life.

Seek purpose.

John Maxwell, the Christian pastor, author, and motivational speaker, visited with us at Cardinals' spring training. One insight left a powerful mark on me: "Everything worth fighting for is uphill."

The wisdom in this thought is impossible to deny, and it got me thinking about my personal situation.

Even after battling against long odds to make it to the big leagues and accumulating various accolades, I often found myself wondering, *What have I really accomplished? Why did I do all that? And what is my true purpose?*

We all have different belief systems, but I believe that God puts us all on this earth with an intended purpose, and I believe that He allowed me to successfully chase my dream and keep the faith through all my challenges so that I would come out the other side prepared to inspire others—to offer a tangible object lesson about battling through adversity.

This is one of the reasons why I wrote the book you are holding in your hands.

Everybody has a story. What are you doing with yours? What is your purpose?

Only you can figure that out, but the sooner you do, the sooner you start chasing some sort of deeper meaning in your life, the more fulfilled you will be.

Source Notes

UNLESS OTHERWISE INDICATED, ALL direct quotes were taken from the author's memory or from personal interviews.

1. "Memorial Hall...silently teaches..." Naval Academy website.

2. "Now colleges from sea to sea..." Naval Academy website.

3. "Mitch is simply...", *NavySports.com*, August 30, 2006.

4. "He's very appreciative...", Russ Charpentier, *Cape Cod Times*, June 22, 2007.

5. "I was surprised...", Russ Charpentier, *Cape Cod Times*, June 22, 2007.

6. "[The Navy doesn't] want to take...", Russ Charpentier, *Cape Cod Times*, June 22, 2007.

7. "When the nation is not...", Memorandum for Chief of Naval Operations, November 2, 2007.

8. "I can't even put into words...", *StateCollege.com*, June 22, 2013.

9. "I couldn't have written...", *Centre Daily Times*, August 31, 2013.

10. "Obviously I'm pumped...", Kary Booher, *Springfield*

News-Leader, May 26, 2014.

11. "From where he was...", *Sports Illustrated*, October 28, 2014.

12. "There's no doubt the younger...", *Sports Illustrated*, October 28, 2014.

13. "There are a lot...", *MLB.com*, April 25, 2015.

14. "For all we do...", *USA TODAY*, May 21, 2015.

15. "Years from now...", *Associated Press*, September 5, 2016.